ISBN 0-8373-4086-1
C-4086   CAREER EXAMINATION SERIES

This is your
PASSBOOK® for...

Traffic Engineer III

Test Preparation Study Guide
Questions & Answers

NLC

NATIONAL LEARNING CORPORATION

PASSBOOK®

NOTICE

PASSBOOK SERIES®

THE *PASSBOOK SERIES®* has been created to prepare applicants and candidates for the ultimate academic battlefield – the examination room.

At some time in our lives, each and every one of us may be required to take an examination – for validation, matriculation, admission, qualification, registration, certification, or licensure.

Based on the assumption that every applicant or candidate has met the basic formal educational standards, has taken the required number of courses, and read the necessary texts, the *PASSBOOK SERIES®* furnishes the one special preparation which may assure passing with confidence, instead of failing with insecurity. Examination questions – together with answers – are furnished as the basic vehicle for study so that the mysteries of the examination and its compounding difficulties may be eliminated or diminished by a sure method.

This book is meant to help you pass your examination provided that you qualify and are serious in your objective.

The entire field is reviewed through the huge store of content information which is succinctly presented through a provocative and challenging approach – the question-and-answer method.

A climate of success is established by furnishing the correct answers at the end of each test.

You soon learn to recognize types of questions, forms of questions, and patterns of questioning. You may even begin to anticipate expected outcomes.

You perceive that many questions are repeated or adapted so that you can gain acute insights, which may enable you to score many sure points.

You learn how to confront new questions, or types of questions, and to attack them confidently and work out the correct answers.

You note objectives and emphases, and recognize pitfalls and dangers, so that you may make positive educational adjustments.

Moreover, you are kept fully informed in relation to new concepts, methods, practices, and directions in the field.

You discover that you are actually taking the examination all the time: you are preparing for the examination by "taking" an examination, not by reading extraneous and/or supererogatory textbooks.

In short, this PASSBOOK®, used directedly, should be an important factor in helping you to pass your test.

TRAFFIC ENGINEER III

DUTIES
Under general supervision, an employee in this class plans and supervises the activities of a traffic engineering work section. Work entails the application of traffic engineering skills and knowledge on various projects. Work is reviewed by a supervisor through discussions and inspections, principally for determining general progress and adherence to departmental policies and regulations. Supervision is exercised over a staff of Traffic Engineers and Traffic Technicians. Does related work as required.

SCOPE OF THE EXAMINATION
The <u>written test</u> will cover knowledge, skills and/or abilities in such areas as:

1. Engineering plans, specifications and estimates;
2. Preparing written material;
3. Supervision;
4. Principles and practices of traffic and transportation engineering;
5. Traffic control devices and regulations, and collection, analysis and presentation of data; and
6. Highway planning, design, safety and laws.

HOW TO TAKE A TEST

I. YOU MUST PASS AN EXAMINATION

A. *WHAT EVERY CANDIDATE SHOULD KNOW*

Examination applicants often ask us for help in preparing for the written test. What can I study in advance? What kinds of questions will be asked? How will the test be given? How will the papers be graded?

As an applicant for a civil service examination, you may be wondering about some of these things. Our purpose here is to suggest effective methods of advance study and to describe civil service examinations.

Your chances for success on this examination can be increased if you know how to prepare. Those "pre-examination jitters" can be reduced if you know what to expect. You can even experience an adventure in good citizenship if you know why civil service exams are given.

B. *WHY ARE CIVIL SERVICE EXAMINATIONS GIVEN?*

Civil service examinations are important to you in two ways. As a citizen, you want public jobs filled by employees who know how to do their work. As a job seeker, you want a fair chance to compete for that job on an equal footing with other candidates. The best-known means of accomplishing this two-fold goal is the competitive examination.

Exams are widely publicized throughout the nation. They may be administered for jobs in federal, state, city, municipal, town or village governments or agencies.

Any citizen may apply, with some limitations, such as the age or residence of applicants. Your experience and education may be reviewed to see whether you meet the requirements for the particular examination. When these requirements exist, they are reasonable and applied consistently to all applicants. Thus, a competitive examination may cause you some uneasiness now, but it is your privilege and safeguard.

C. *HOW ARE CIVIL SERVICE EXAMS DEVELOPED?*

Examinations are carefully written by trained technicians who are specialists in the field known as "psychological measurement," in consultation with recognized authorities in the field of work that the test will cover. These experts recommend the subject matter areas or skills to be tested; only those knowledges or skills important to your success on the job are included. The most reliable books and source materials available are used as references. Together, the experts and technicians judge the difficulty level of the questions.

Test technicians know how to phrase questions so that the problem is clearly stated. Their ethics do not permit "trick" or "catch" questions. Questions may have been tried out on sample groups, or subjected to statistical analysis, to determine their usefulness.

Written tests are often used in combination with performance tests, ratings of training and experience, and oral interviews. All of these measures combine to form the best-known means of finding the right person for the right job.

II. HOW TO PASS THE WRITTEN TEST

A. NATURE OF THE EXAMINATION

To prepare intelligently for civil service examinations, you should know how they differ from school examinations you have taken. In school you were assigned certain definite pages to read or subjects to cover. The examination questions were quite detailed and usually emphasized memory. Civil service exams, on the other hand, try to discover your present ability to perform the duties of a position, plus your potentiality to learn these duties. In other words, a civil service exam attempts to predict how successful you will be. Questions cover such a broad area that they cannot be as minute and detailed as school exam questions.

In the public service similar kinds of work, or positions, are grouped together in one "class." This process is known as *position-classification*. All the positions in a class are paid according to the salary range for that class. One class title covers all of these positions, and they are all tested by the same examination.

B. FOUR BASIC STEPS

1) Study the announcement

How, then, can you know what subjects to study? Our best answer is: "Learn as much as possible about the class of positions for which you've applied." The exam will test the knowledge, skills and abilities needed to do the work.

Your most valuable source of information about the position you want is the official exam announcement. This announcement lists the training and experience qualifications. Check these standards and apply only if you come reasonably close to meeting them.

The brief description of the position in the examination announcement offers some clues to the subjects which will be tested. Think about the job itself. Review the duties in your mind. Can you perform them, or are there some in which you are rusty? Fill in the blank spots in your preparation.

Many jurisdictions preview the written test in the exam announcement by including a section called "Knowledge and Abilities Required," "Scope of the Examination," or some similar heading. Here you will find out specifically what fields will be tested.

2) Review your own background

Once you learn in general what the position is all about, and what you need to know to do the work, ask yourself which subjects you already know fairly well and which need improvement. You may wonder whether to concentrate on improving your strong areas or on building some background in your fields of weakness. When the announcement has specified "some knowledge" or "considerable knowledge," or has used adjectives like "beginning principles of…" or "advanced … methods," you can get a clue as to the number and difficulty of questions to be asked in any given field. More questions, and hence broader coverage, would be included for those subjects which are more important in the work. Now weigh your strengths and weaknesses against the job requirements and prepare accordingly.

3) Determine the level of the position

Another way to tell how intensively you should prepare is to understand the level of the job for which you are applying. Is it the entering level? In other words, is this the position in which beginners in a field of work are hired? Or is it an intermediate or advanced level? Sometimes this is indicated by such words as "Junior" or "Senior" in the class title. Other jurisdictions use Roman numerals to designate the level – Clerk I, Clerk II, for example. The word "Supervisor" sometimes appears in the title. If the level is not indicated by the title, check the description of duties. Will you be working under very close supervision, or will you have responsibility for independent decisions in this work?

4) Choose appropriate study materials

Now that you know the subjects to be examined and the relative amount of each subject to be covered, you can choose suitable study materials. For beginning level jobs, or even advanced ones, if you have a pronounced weakness in some aspect of your training, read a modern, standard textbook in that field. Be sure it is up to date and has general coverage. Such books are normally available at your library, and the librarian will be glad to help you locate one. For entry-level positions, questions of appropriate difficulty are chosen – neither highly advanced questions, nor those too simple. Such questions require careful thought but not advanced training.

If the position for which you are applying is technical or advanced, you will read more advanced, specialized material. If you are already familiar with the basic principles of your field, elementary textbooks would waste your time. Concentrate on advanced textbooks and technical periodicals. Think through the concepts and review difficult problems in your field.

These are all general sources. You can get more ideas on your own initiative, following these leads. For example, training manuals and publications of the government agency which employs workers in your field can be useful, particularly for technical and professional positions. A letter or visit to the government department involved may result in more specific study suggestions, and certainly will provide you with a more definite idea of the exact nature of the position you are seeking.

III. KINDS OF TESTS

Tests are used for purposes other than measuring knowledge and ability to perform specified duties. For some positions, it is equally important to test ability to make adjustments to new situations or to profit from training. In others, basic mental abilities not dependent on information are essential. Questions which test these things may not appear as pertinent to the duties of the position as those which test for knowledge and information. Yet they are often highly important parts of a fair examination. For very general questions, it is almost impossible to help you direct your study efforts. What we can do is to point out some of the more common of these general abilities needed in public service positions and describe some typical questions.

1) General information

Broad, general information has been found useful for predicting job success in some kinds of work. This is tested in a variety of ways, from vocabulary lists to questions about current events. Basic background in some field of work, such as sociology or economics, may be sampled in a group of questions. Often these are principles which have become familiar to most persons through exposure rather than through formal training. It is difficult to advise you how to study for these questions; being alert to the world around you is our best suggestion.

2) Verbal ability

An example of an ability needed in many positions is verbal or language ability. Verbal ability is, in brief, the ability to use and understand words. Vocabulary and grammar tests are typical measures of this ability. Reading comprehension or paragraph interpretation questions are common in many kinds of civil service tests. You are given a paragraph of written material and asked to find its central meaning.

3) Numerical ability

Number skills can be tested by the familiar arithmetic problem, by checking paired lists of numbers to see which are alike and which are different, or by interpreting charts and graphs. In the latter test, a graph may be printed in the test booklet which you are asked to use as the basis for answering questions.

4) Observation

A popular test for law-enforcement positions is the observation test. A picture is shown to you for several minutes, then taken away. Questions about the picture test your ability to observe both details and larger elements.

5) Following directions

In many positions in the public service, the employee must be able to carry out written instructions dependably and accurately. You may be given a chart with several columns, each column listing a variety of information. The questions require you to carry out directions involving the information given in the chart.

6) Skills and aptitudes

Performance tests effectively measure some manual skills and aptitudes. When the skill is one in which you are trained, such as typing or shorthand, you can practice. These tests are often very much like those given in business school or high school courses. For many of the other skills and aptitudes, however, no short-time preparation can be made. Skills and abilities natural to you or that you have developed throughout your lifetime are being tested.

Many of the general questions just described provide all the data needed to answer the questions and ask you to use your reasoning ability to find the answers. Your best preparation for these tests, as well as for tests of facts and ideas, is to be at your physical and mental best. You, no doubt, have your own methods of getting into an exam-taking mood and keeping "in shape." The next section lists some ideas on this subject.

IV. KINDS OF QUESTIONS

Only rarely is the "essay" question, which you answer in narrative form, used in civil service tests. Civil service tests are usually of the short-answer type. Full instructions for answering these questions will be given to you at the examination. But in case this is your first experience with short-answer questions and separate answer sheets, here is what you need to know:

1) Multiple-choice Questions

Most popular of the short-answer questions is the "multiple choice" or "best answer" question. It can be used, for example, to test for factual knowledge, ability to solve problems or judgment in meeting situations found at work.

A multiple-choice question is normally one of three types—

- It can begin with an incomplete statement followed by several possible endings. You are to find the one ending which *best* completes the statement, although some of the others may not be entirely wrong.
- It can also be a complete statement in the form of a question which is answered by choosing one of the statements listed.
- It can be in the form of a problem – again you select the best answer.

Here is an example of a multiple-choice question with a discussion which should give you some clues as to the method for choosing the right answer:

When an employee has a complaint about his assignment, the action which will *best* help him overcome his difficulty is to
  A. discuss his difficulty with his coworkers
  B. take the problem to the head of the organization
  C. take the problem to the person who gave him the assignment
  D. say nothing to anyone about his complaint

In answering this question, you should study each of the choices to find which is best. Consider choice "A" – Certainly an employee may discuss his complaint with fellow employees, but no change or improvement can result, and the complaint remains unresolved. Choice "B" is a poor choice since the head of the organization probably does not know what assignment you have been given, and taking your problem to him is known as "going over the head" of the supervisor. The supervisor, or person who made the assignment, is the person who can clarify it or correct any injustice. Choice "C" is, therefore, correct. To say nothing, as in choice "D," is unwise. Supervisors have and interest in knowing the problems employees are facing, and the employee is seeking a solution to his problem.

2) True/False Questions

The "true/false" or "right/wrong" form of question is sometimes used. Here a complete statement is given. Your job is to decide whether the statement is right or wrong.

SAMPLE: A person-to-person long-distance telephone call costs less than a station-to-station call to the same city.

This statement is wrong, or false, since person-to-person calls are more expensive.

This is not a complete list of all possible question forms, although most of the others are variations of these common types. You will always get complete directions for answering questions. Be sure you understand *how* to mark your answers – ask questions until you do.

V. RECORDING YOUR ANSWERS

For an examination with very few applicants, you may be told to record your answers in the test booklet itself. Separate answer sheets are much more common. If this separate answer sheet is to be scored by machine – and this is often the case – it is highly important that you mark your answers correctly in order to get credit.

An electric scoring machine is often used in civil service offices because of the speed with which papers can be scored. Machine-scored answer sheets must be marked with a pencil, which will be given to you. This pencil has a high graphite content which responds to the electric scoring machine. As a matter of fact, stray dots may register as answers, so do not let your pencil rest on the answer sheet while you are pondering the correct answer. Also, if your pencil lead breaks or is otherwise defective, ask for another.

Since the answer sheet will be dropped in a slot in the scoring machine, be careful not to bend the corners or get the paper crumpled.

The answer sheet normally has five vertical columns of numbers, with 30 numbers to a column. These numbers correspond to the question numbers in your test booklet. After each number, going across the page are four or five pairs of dotted lines. These short dotted lines have small letters or numbers above them. The first two pairs may also have a "T" or "F" above the letters. This indicates that the first two pairs only are to be used if the questions are of the true-false type. If the questions are multiple choice, disregard the "T" and "F" and pay attention only to the small letters or numbers.

Answer your questions in the manner of the sample that follows:

32. The largest city in the United States is
   A. Washington, D.C.
   B. New York City
   C. Chicago
   D. Detroit
   E. San Francisco

1) Choose the answer you think is best. (New York City is the largest, so "B" is correct.)
2) Find the row of dotted lines numbered the same as the question you are answering. (Find row number 32)
3) Find the pair of dotted lines corresponding to the answer. (Find the pair of lines under the mark "B.")
4) Make a solid black mark between the dotted lines.

VI. BEFORE THE TEST

Common sense will help you find procedures to follow to get ready for an examination. Too many of us, however, overlook these sensible measures. Indeed, nervousness and fatigue have been found to be the most serious reasons why applicants fail to do their best on civil service tests. Here is a list of reminders:

- Begin your preparation early – Don't wait until the last minute to go scurrying around for books and materials or to find out what the position is all about.
- Prepare continuously – An hour a night for a week is better than an all-night cram session. This has been definitely established. What is more, a night a

6

week for a month will return better dividends than crowding your study into a shorter period of time.

- Locate the place of the exam – You have been sent a notice telling you when and where to report for the examination. If the location is in a different town or otherwise unfamiliar to you, it would be well to inquire the best route and learn something about the building.
- Relax the night before the test – Allow your mind to rest. Do not study at all that night. Plan some mild recreation or diversion; then go to bed early and get a good night's sleep.
- Get up early enough to make a leisurely trip to the place for the test – This way unforeseen events, traffic snarls, unfamiliar buildings, etc. will not upset you.
- Dress comfortably – A written test is not a fashion show. You will be known by number and not by name, so wear something comfortable.
- Leave excess paraphernalia at home – Shopping bags and odd bundles will get in your way. You need bring only the items mentioned in the official notice you received; usually everything you need is provided. Do not bring reference books to the exam. They will only confuse those last minutes and be taken away from you when in the test room.
- Arrive somewhat ahead of time – If because of transportation schedules you must get there very early, bring a newspaper or magazine to take your mind off yourself while waiting.
- Locate the examination room – When you have found the proper room, you will be directed to the seat or part of the room where you will sit. Sometimes you are given a sheet of instructions to read while you are waiting. Do not fill out any forms until you are told to do so; just read them and be prepared.
- Relax and prepare to listen to the instructions
- If you have any physical problem that may keep you from doing your best, be sure to tell the test administrator. If you are sick or in poor health, you really cannot do your best on the exam. You can come back and take the test some other time.

VII. AT THE TEST

The day of the test is here and you have the test booklet in your hand. The temptation to get going is very strong. Caution! There is more to success than knowing the right answers. You must know how to identify your papers and understand variations in the type of short-answer question used in this particular examination. Follow these suggestions for maximum results from your efforts:

1) Cooperate with the monitor

The test administrator has a duty to create a situation in which you can be as much at ease as possible. He will give instructions, tell you when to begin, check to see that you are marking your answer sheet correctly, and so on. He is not there to guard you, although he will see that your competitors do not take unfair advantage. He wants to help you do your best.

2) Listen to all instructions

Don't jump the gun! Wait until you understand all directions. In most civil service tests you get more time than you need to answer the questions. So don't be in a hurry.

Read each word of instructions until you clearly understand the meaning. Study the examples, listen to all announcements and follow directions. Ask questions if you do not understand what to do.

3) Identify your papers

Civil service exams are usually identified by number only. You will be assigned a number; you must not put your name on your test papers. Be sure to copy your number correctly. Since more than one exam may be given, copy your exact examination title.

4) Plan your time

Unless you are told that a test is a "speed" or "rate of work" test, speed itself is usually not important. Time enough to answer all the questions will be provided, but this does not mean that you have all day. An overall time limit has been set. Divide the total time (in minutes) by the number of questions to determine the approximate time you have for each question.

5) Do not linger over difficult questions

If you come across a difficult question, mark it with a paper clip (useful to have along) and come back to it when you have been through the booklet. One caution if you do this – be sure to skip a number on your answer sheet as well. Check often to be sure that you have not lost your place and that you are marking in the row numbered the same as the question you are answering.

6) Read the questions

Be sure you know what the question asks! Many capable people are unsuccessful because they failed to *read* the questions correctly.

7) Answer all questions

Unless you have been instructed that a penalty will be deducted for incorrect answers, it is better to guess than to omit a question.

8) Speed tests

It is often better NOT to guess on speed tests. It has been found that on timed tests people are tempted to spend the last few seconds before time is called in marking answers at random – without even reading them – in the hope of picking up a few extra points. To discourage this practice, the instructions may warn you that your score will be "corrected" for guessing. That is, a penalty will be applied. The incorrect answers will be deducted from the correct ones, or some other penalty formula will be used.

9) Review your answers

If you finish before time is called, go back to the questions you guessed or omitted to give them further thought. Review other answers if you have time.

10) Return your test materials

If you are ready to leave before others have finished or time is called, take ALL your materials to the monitor and leave quietly. Never take any test material with you. The monitor can discover whose papers are not complete, and taking a test booklet may be grounds for disqualification.

VIII. EXAMINATION TECHNIQUES

1) Read the general instructions carefully. These are usually printed on the first page of the exam booklet. As a rule, these instructions refer to the timing of the examination; the fact that you should not start work until the signal and must stop work at a signal, etc. If there are any *special* instructions, such as a choice of questions to be answered, make sure that you note this instruction carefully.

2) When you are ready to start work on the examination, that is as soon as the signal has been given, read the instructions to each question booklet, underline any key words or phrases, such as *least, best, outline, describe* and the like. In this way you will tend to answer as requested rather than discover on reviewing your paper that you *listed without describing*, that you selected the *worst* choice rather than the *best* choice, etc.

3) If the examination is of the objective or multiple-choice type – that is, each question will also give a series of possible answers: A, B, C or D, and you are called upon to select the best answer and write the letter next to that answer on your answer paper – it is advisable to start answering each question in turn. There may be anywhere from 50 to 100 such questions in the three or four hours allotted and you can see how much time would be taken if you read through all the questions before beginning to answer any. Furthermore, if you come across a question or group of questions which you know would be difficult to answer, it would undoubtedly affect your handling of all the other questions.

4) If the examination is of the essay type and contains but a few questions, it is a moot point as to whether you should read all the questions before starting to answer any one. Of course, if you are given a choice – say five out of seven and the like – then it is essential to read all the questions so you can eliminate the two that are most difficult. If, however, you are asked to answer all the questions, there may be danger in trying to answer the easiest one first because you may find that you will spend too much time on it. The best technique is to answer the first question, then proceed to the second, etc.

5) Time your answers. Before the exam begins, write down the time it started, then add the time allowed for the examination and write down the time it must be completed, then divide the time available somewhat as follows:
   - If 3-1/2 hours are allowed, that would be 210 minutes. If you have 80 objective-type questions, that would be an average of 2-1/2 minutes per question. Allow yourself no more than 2 minutes per question, or a total of 160 minutes, which will permit about 50 minutes to review.
   - If for the time allotment of 210 minutes there are 7 essay questions to answer, that would average about 30 minutes a question. Give yourself only 25 minutes per question so that you have about 35 minutes to review.

6) The most important instruction is to *read each question* and make sure you know what is wanted. The second most important instruction is to *time yourself properly* so that you answer every question. The third most

important instruction is to *answer every question*. Guess if you have to but include something for each question. Remember that you will receive no credit for a blank and will probably receive some credit if you write something in answer to an essay question. If you guess a letter – say "B" for a multiple-choice question – you may have guessed right. If you leave a blank as an answer to a multiple-choice question, the examiners may respect your feelings but it will not add a point to your score. Some exams may penalize you for wrong answers, so in such cases *only*, you may not want to guess unless you have some basis for your answer.

7) Suggestions
   a. Objective-type questions
      1. Examine the question booklet for proper sequence of pages and questions
      2. Read all instructions carefully
      3. Skip any question which seems too difficult; return to it after all other questions have been answered
      4. Apportion your time properly; do not spend too much time on any single question or group of questions
      5. Note and underline key words – *all, most, fewest, least, best, worst, same, opposite,* etc.
      6. Pay particular attention to negatives
      7. Note unusual option, e.g., unduly long, short, complex, different or similar in content to the body of the question
      8. Observe the use of "hedging" words – *probably, may, most likely,* etc.
      9. Make sure that your answer is put next to the same number as the question
      10. Do not second-guess unless you have good reason to believe the second answer is definitely more correct
      11. Cross out original answer if you decide another answer is more accurate; do not erase until you are ready to hand your paper in
      12. Answer all questions; guess unless instructed otherwise
      13. Leave time for review

   b. Essay questions
      1. Read each question carefully
      2. Determine exactly what is wanted. Underline key words or phrases.
      3. Decide on outline or paragraph answer
      4. Include many different points and elements unless asked to develop any one or two points or elements
      5. Show impartiality by giving pros and cons unless directed to select one side only
      6. Make and write down any assumptions you find necessary to answer the questions
      7. Watch your English, grammar, punctuation and choice of words
      8. Time your answers; don't crowd material

8) Answering the essay question

Most essay questions can be answered by framing the specific response around several key words or ideas. Here are a few such key words or ideas:

M's: manpower, materials, methods, money, management
P's: purpose, program, policy, plan, procedure, practice, problems, pitfalls, personnel, public relations

    a. Six basic steps in handling problems:
1. Preliminary plan and background development
2. Collect information, data and facts
3. Analyze and interpret information, data and facts
4. Analyze and develop solutions as well as make recommendations
5. Prepare report and sell recommendations
6. Install recommendations and follow up effectiveness

    b. Pitfalls to avoid
1. *Taking things for granted* – A statement of the situation does not necessarily imply that each of the elements is necessarily true; for example, a complaint may be invalid and biased so that all that can be taken for granted is that a complaint has been registered
2. *Considering only one side of a situation* – Wherever possible, indicate several alternatives and then point out the reasons you selected the best one
3. *Failing to indicate follow up* – Whenever your answer indicates action on your part, make certain that you will take proper follow-up action to see how successful your recommendations, procedures or actions turn out to be
4. *Taking too long in answering any single question* – Remember to time your answers properly

IX. AFTER THE TEST

    Scoring procedures differ in detail among civil service jurisdictions although the general principles are the same. Whether the papers are hand-scored or graded by machine we have described, they are nearly always graded by number. That is, the person who marks the paper knows only the number – never the name – of the applicant. Not until all the papers have been graded will they be matched with names. If other tests, such as training and experience or oral interview ratings have been given, scores will be combined. Different parts of the examination usually have different weights. For example, the written test might count 60 percent of the final grade, and a rating of training and experience 40 percent. In many jurisdictions, veterans will have a certain number of points added to their grades.

    After the final grade has been determined, the names are placed in grade order and an eligible list is established. There are various methods for resolving ties between those who get the same final grade – probably the most common is to place first the name of the person whose application was received first. Job offers are made from the eligible list in the order the names appear on it. You will be notified of your grade and your rank as soon as all these computations have been made. This will be done as rapidly as possible.

    People who are found to meet the requirements in the announcement are called "eligibles." Their names are put on a list of eligible candidates. An eligible's chances of getting a job depend on how high he stands on this list and how fast agencies are filling jobs from the list.

When a job is to be filled from a list of eligibles, the agency asks for the names of people on the list of eligibles for that job. When the civil service commission receives this request, it sends to the agency the names of the three people highest on this list. Or, if the job to be filled has specialized requirements, the office sends the agency the names of the top three persons who meet these requirements from the general list.

The appointing officer makes a choice from among the three people whose names were sent to him. If the selected person accepts the appointment, the names of the others are put back on the list to be considered for future openings.

That is the rule in hiring from all kinds of eligible lists, whether they are for typist, carpenter, chemist, or something else. For every vacancy, the appointing officer has his choice of any one of the top three eligibles on the list. This explains why the person whose name is on top of the list sometimes does not get an appointment when some of the persons lower on the list do. If the appointing officer chooses the second or third eligible, the No. 1 eligible does not get a job at once, but stays on the list until he is appointed or the list is terminated.

X. HOW TO PASS THE INTERVIEW TEST

The examination for which you applied requires an oral interview test. You have already taken the written test and you are now being called for the interview test – the final part of the formal examination.

You may think that it is not possible to prepare for an interview test and that there are no procedures to follow during an interview. Our purpose is to point out some things you can do in advance that will help you and some good rules to follow and pitfalls to avoid while you are being interviewed.

What is an interview supposed to test?

The written examination is designed to test the technical knowledge and competence of the candidate; the oral is designed to evaluate intangible qualities, not readily measured otherwise, and to establish a list showing the relative fitness of each candidate – as measured against his competitors – for the position sought. Scoring is not on the basis of "right" and "wrong," but on a sliding scale of values ranging from "not passable" to "outstanding." As a matter of fact, it is possible to achieve a relatively low score without a single "incorrect" answer because of evident weakness in the qualities being measured.

Occasionally, an examination may consist entirely of an oral test – either an individual or a group oral. In such cases, information is sought concerning the technical knowledges and abilities of the candidate, since there has been no written examination for this purpose. More commonly, however, an oral test is used to supplement a written examination.

Who conducts interviews?

The composition of oral boards varies among different jurisdictions. In nearly all, a representative of the personnel department serves as chairman. One of the members of the board may be a representative of the department in which the candidate would work. In some cases, "outside experts" are used, and, frequently, a businessman or some other representative of the general public is asked to serve. Labor and management or other special groups may be represented. The aim is to secure the services of experts in the appropriate field.

However the board is composed, it is a good idea (and not at all improper or unethical) to ascertain in advance of the interview who the members are and what groups they represent. When you are introduced to them, you will have some idea of their backgrounds and interests, and at least you will not stutter and stammer over their names.

What should be done before the interview?

While knowledge about the board members is useful and takes some of the surprise element out of the interview, there is other preparation which is more substantive. It *is* possible to prepare for an oral interview – in several ways:

1) Keep a copy of your application and review it carefully before the interview

This may be the only document before the oral board, and the starting point of the interview. Know what education and experience you have listed there, and the sequence and dates of all of it. Sometimes the board will ask you to review the highlights of your experience for them; you should not have to hem and haw doing it.

2) Study the class specification and the examination announcement

Usually, the oral board has one or both of these to guide them. The qualities, characteristics or knowledges required by the position sought are stated in these documents. They offer valuable clues as to the nature of the oral interview. For example, if the job involves supervisory responsibilities, the announcement will usually indicate that knowledge of modern supervisory methods and the qualifications of the candidate as a supervisor will be tested. If so, you can expect such questions, frequently in the form of a hypothetical situation which you are expected to solve. NEVER go into an oral without knowledge of the duties and responsibilities of the job you seek.

3) Think through each qualification required

Try to visualize the kind of questions you would ask if you were a board member. How well could you answer them? Try especially to appraise your own knowledge and background in each area, *measured against the job sought*, and identify any areas in which you are weak. Be critical and realistic – do not flatter yourself.

4) Do some general reading in areas in which you feel you may be weak

For example, if the job involves supervision and your past experience has NOT, some general reading in supervisory methods and practices, particularly in the field of human relations, might be useful. Do NOT study agency procedures or detailed manuals. The oral board will be testing your understanding and capacity, not your memory.

5) Get a good night's sleep and watch your general health and mental attitude

You will want a clear head at the interview. Take care of a cold or any other minor ailment, and of course, no hangovers.

What should be done on the day of the interview?

Now comes the day of the interview itself. Give yourself plenty of time to get there. Plan to arrive somewhat ahead of the scheduled time, particularly if your appointment is in the fore part of the day. If a previous candidate fails to appear, the board might be ready for you a bit early. By early afternoon an oral board is almost invariably behind schedule if there are many candidates, and you may have to wait.

Take along a book or magazine to read, or your application to review, but leave any extraneous material in the waiting room when you go in for your interview. In any event, relax and compose yourself.

The matter of dress is important. The board is forming impressions about you – from your experience, your manners, your attitude, and your appearance. Give your personal appearance careful attention. Dress your best, but not your flashiest. Choose conservative, appropriate clothing, and be sure it is immaculate. This is a business interview, and your appearance should indicate that you regard it as such. Besides, being well groomed and properly dressed will help boost your confidence.

Sooner or later, someone will call your name and escort you into the interview room. *This is it.* From here on you are on your own. It is too late for any more preparation. But remember, you asked for this opportunity to prove your fitness, and you are here because your request was granted.

What happens when you go in?

The usual sequence of events will be as follows: The clerk (who is often the board stenographer) will introduce you to the chairman of the oral board, who will introduce you to the other members of the board. Acknowledge the introductions before you sit down. Do not be surprised if you find a microphone facing you or a stenotypist sitting by. Oral interviews are usually recorded in the event of an appeal or other review.

Usually the chairman of the board will open the interview by reviewing the highlights of your education and work experience from your application – primarily for the benefit of the other members of the board, as well as to get the material into the record. Do not interrupt or comment unless there is an error or significant misinterpretation; if that is the case, do not hesitate. But do not quibble about insignificant matters. Also, he will usually ask you some question about your education, experience or your present job – partly to get you to start talking and to establish the interviewing "rapport." He may start the actual questioning, or turn it over to one of the other members. Frequently, each member undertakes the questioning on a particular area, one in which he is perhaps most competent, so you can expect each member to participate in the examination. Because time is limited, you may also expect some rather abrupt switches in the direction the questioning takes, so do not be upset by it. Normally, a board member will not pursue a single line of questioning unless he discovers a particular strength or weakness.

After each member has participated, the chairman will usually ask whether any member has any further questions, then will ask you if you have anything you wish to add. Unless you are expecting this question, it may floor you. Worse, it may start you off on an extended, extemporaneous speech. The board is not usually seeking more information. The question is principally to offer you a last opportunity to present further qualifications or to indicate that you have nothing to add. So, if you feel that a significant qualification or characteristic has been overlooked, it is proper to point it out in a sentence or so. Do not compliment the board on the thoroughness of their examination – they have been sketchy, and you know it. If you wish, merely say, "No thank you, I have nothing further to add." This is a point where you can "talk yourself out" of a good impression or fail to present an important bit of information. Remember, *you close the interview yourself.*

The chairman will then say, "That is all, Mr. _____, thank you." Do not be startled; the interview is over, and quicker than you think. Thank him, gather your belongings and take your leave. Save your sigh of relief for the other side of the door.

How to put your best foot forward

Throughout this entire process, you may feel that the board individually and collectively is trying to pierce your defenses, seek out your hidden weaknesses and embarrass and confuse you. Actually, this is not true. They are obliged to make an appraisal of your qualifications for the job you are seeking, and they want to see you in your best light. Remember, they must interview all candidates and a non-cooperative candidate may become a failure in spite of their best efforts to bring out his qualifications. Here are 15 suggestions that will help you:

1) Be natural – Keep your attitude confident, not cocky

If you are not confident that you can do the job, do not expect the board to be. Do not apologize for your weaknesses, try to bring out your strong points. The board is interested in a positive, not negative, presentation. Cockiness will antagonize any board member and make him wonder if you are covering up a weakness by a false show of strength.

2) Get comfortable, but don't lounge or sprawl

Sit erectly but not stiffly. A careless posture may lead the board to conclude that you are careless in other things, or at least that you are not impressed by the importance of the occasion. Either conclusion is natural, even if incorrect. Do not fuss with your clothing, a pencil or an ashtray. Your hands may occasionally be useful to emphasize a point; do not let them become a point of distraction.

3) Do not wisecrack or make small talk

This is a serious situation, and your attitude should show that you consider it as such. Further, the time of the board is limited – they do not want to waste it, and neither should you.

4) Do not exaggerate your experience or abilities

In the first place, from information in the application or other interviews and sources, the board may know more about you than you think. Secondly, you probably will not get away with it. An experienced board is rather adept at spotting such a situation, so do not take the chance.

5) If you know a board member, do not make a point of it, yet do not hide it

Certainly you are not fooling him, and probably not the other members of the board. Do not try to take advantage of your acquaintanceship – it will probably do you little good.

6) Do not dominate the interview

Let the board do that. They will give you the clues – do not assume that you have to do all the talking. Realize that the board has a number of questions to ask you, and do not try to take up all the interview time by showing off your extensive knowledge of the answer to the first one.

7) Be attentive

You only have 20 minutes or so, and you should keep your attention at its sharpest throughout. When a member is addressing a problem or question to you, give him your undivided attention. Address your reply principally to him, but do not exclude the other board members.

8) Do not interrupt

A board member may be stating a problem for you to analyze. He will ask you a question when the time comes. Let him state the problem, and wait for the question.

9) Make sure you understand the question

Do not try to answer until you are sure what the question is. If it is not clear, restate it in your own words or ask the board member to clarify it for you. However, do not haggle about minor elements.

10) Reply promptly but not hastily

A common entry on oral board rating sheets is "candidate responded readily," or "candidate hesitated in replies." Respond as promptly and quickly as you can, but do not jump to a hasty, ill-considered answer.

11) Do not be peremptory in your answers

A brief answer is proper – but do not fire your answer back. That is a losing game from your point of view. The board member can probably ask questions much faster than you can answer them.

12) Do not try to create the answer you think the board member wants

He is interested in what kind of mind you have and how it works – not in playing games. Furthermore, he can usually spot this practice and will actually grade you down on it.

13) Do not switch sides in your reply merely to agree with a board member

Frequently, a member will take a contrary position merely to draw you out and to see if you are willing and able to defend your point of view. Do not start a debate, yet do not surrender a good position. If a position is worth taking, it is worth defending.

14) Do not be afraid to admit an error in judgment if you are shown to be wrong

The board knows that you are forced to reply without any opportunity for careful consideration. Your answer may be demonstrably wrong. If so, admit it and get on with the interview.

15) Do not dwell at length on your present job

The opening question may relate to your present assignment. Answer the question but do not go into an extended discussion. You are being examined for a *new* job, not your present one. As a matter of fact, try to phrase ALL your answers in terms of the job for which you are being examined.

Basis of Rating

Probably you will forget most of these "do's" and "don'ts" when you walk into the oral interview room. Even remembering them all will not ensure you a passing grade. Perhaps you did not have the qualifications in the first place. But remembering them will help you to put your best foot forward, without treading on the toes of the board members.

Rumor and popular opinion to the contrary notwithstanding, an oral board wants you to make the best appearance possible. They know you are under pressure – but they also want to see how you respond to it as a guide to what your reaction would be under the pressures of the job you seek. They will be influenced by the degree of poise you display, the personal traits you show and the manner in which you respond.

EXAMINATION SECTION

EXAMINATION SECTION
TEST 1

DIRECTIONS: Each question or incomplete statement is followed by several suggested answers or completions. Select the one that BEST answers the question or completes the statement. *PRINT THE LETTER OF THE CORRECT ANSWER IN THE SPACE AT THE RIGHT.*

1. A _____ would MOST likely be used to estimate the cost of additional yards of concrete, or additional lengths of piling.   1.___
   - A. quantity survey
   - B. lump-sum amount
   - C. cost-per-square-foot estimate
   - D. unit cost estimate

2. How many studs are usually required for 10 linear feet of wall, excluding openings and plates?   2.___
   - A. 1   B. 5   C. 10   D. 12

3. What is represented by the mechanical symbol shown at the right?   3.___
   - A. Supply duct   B. Gauge
   - C. Exhaust duct   D. Floor drain

4. The excavation of compacted sand or gravel will require an angle of repose (slope) of 1 ft. vertical to _____ ft. horizontal.   4.___
   - A. 3/4   B. 1   C. 1½   D. 2

5. Which of the following types of tile for resilient flooring would be LEAST expensive?   5.___
   - A. Pure vinyl   B. Asphalt
   - C. Cork   D. Rubberized marbleized

6. What is the typical estimate (in linear feet) for two laborers' output per day of regular chain-link fencing?   6.___
   - A. 50   B. 100   C. 150   D. 200

7. What is used between the ridge and valley rafters of a roof construction?   7.___
   - A. Fascia   B. Hip rafter
   - C. Packing   D. Jack rafter

8. Approximately how many square feet of surface area can be covered by 1 gallon of adhesive for resilient flooring sheet material?   8.___
   - A. 75   B. 125   C. 200   D. 250

9. Water piping is NOT typically made of
   A. copper   B. cast iron
   C. galvanized steel   D. plastic

                                      9.___

10. What is represented by the electrical symbol shown at the right?   10.___
   A. Buzzer   B. Clock receptacle
   C. Electric motor   D. Circuit breaker

11. Approximately how many linear feet of ¼" copper pipe can be installed in a typical work day?   11.___
   A. 35-40   B. 50-60   C. 65-75   D. 85-100

12. What is the term for short studs required beneath window framing, and at similar locations?   12.___
   A. Scrap   B. Cripple   C. Hash   D. Hips

13. For MOST brick work, scaffolding is required at intervals of about _____ feet.   13.___
   A. 4   B. 6   C. 8   D. 10

14. What type of concrete masonry unit is represented by the drawing shown at the right?   14.___
   A. Header
   B. Stretcher
   C. Channel
   D. Bull nose

15. The movable portion of a window that contains the glass is the   15.___
   A. cornice   B. sash   C. scale   D. pane

16. Approximately how many hours of labor will be required for the installation of 100 square feet of countertop ceramic tile and a 6" back splash?   16.___
   A. 3   B. 5   C. 8   D. 12

17. Which of the following types of wall constructions will be LEAST able to dampen the transmission of sound?   17.___
   A. Single-stud gypsum board
   B. Metal-stud plaster on lath
   C. Single-stud plaster on gypsum board
   D. Staggered-stud gypsum board

18. What is represented by the mechanical symbol shown at the right?   18.___
   A. Return duct   B. Shower
   C. Corner tub   D. Water or fuel tank

19. Which of the following types of aluminum windows would be MOST expensive to install?   19.___
   A. Horizontal sliding   B. Casement
   C. Double-hung   D. Projected vent

20. Generally, an adequate interest or profit return from a construction job must be more than _____%.
    A. 3-5   B. 7-10   C. 12-22   D. 24-45   20._____

21. Which of the following types of doors would be LEAST expensive?   21._____
    A. Hollow core, birch-veneer face
    B. Solid-core, walnut-faced
    C. Hollow core, hardboard-faced
    D. Solid-core, birch-veneer face

22. What is represented by the architectural symbol shown at the right?   22._____
    A. Shingle roofing   B. Aluminum
    C. Structural metal   D. Cast iron

23. Approximately how many hours should be estimated for the trimming of a door blank (3'x7' wood door), plus the installation of frame and trim?   23._____
    A. 1   B. 2   C. 4   D. 6

24. Which of the following types of wire enclosures is NOT currently in use?   24._____
    A. Romex   B. Conduit
    C. Flexible cable   D. Knob-in-tube

25. If precut granite block is used for curbs, the cost will be roughly _____% more than the cost for using concrete.   25._____
    A. 10   B. 30   C. 50   D. 70

KEY (CORRECT ANSWERS)

1. D		11. B	
2. C		12. B	
3. A		13. A	
4. C		14. B	
5. B		15. B	
6. C		16. D	
7. D		17. A	
8. C		18. D	
9. B		19. B	
10. C		20. B	

21. C
22. D
23. C
24. D
25. C

TEST 2

DIRECTIONS: Each question or incomplete statement is followed by several suggested answers or completions. Select the one that BEST answers the question or completes the statement. *PRINT THE LETTER OF THE CORRECT ANSWER IN THE SPACE AT THE RIGHT.*

1. In an average work day, approximately how many cubic yards   1.___
    of earth can be excavated by means of a tractor shovel
    with a 1-yard bucket?
    A. 10   B. 75   C. 350   D. 500

2. Mesh reinforcing material is MOST commonly used in   2.___
    A. vertical walls   B. supports
    C. slabs   D. footings

3. What is represented by the architectural   3.___
    symbol shown at the right?
    A. Cut stone   B. Concrete block
    C. Rubble stone   D. Fire brick

4. Which of the following does NOT require an external trap   4.___
    that connects the sewer line?
    A. Kitchen sink   B. Toilet
    C. Lavatory   D. Tub

5. In one hour, a typical caisson boring machine will be   5.___
    able to bore _____ linear feet.
    A. 75   B. 125   C. 200   D. 250

6. Most bath accessories require about _____ to install.   6.___
    A. 15 minutes   B. 45 minutes
    C. 1 hour   D. 1½ hours

7. What is represented by the electrical symbol   7.___
    shown at the right?
    A. Electric motor   B. Bell
    C. Paging system   D. Street light and bracket

8. Which of the following plumbing (pipe) materials would   8.___
    be MOST expensive to install?
    A. 3" galvanized steel   B. ¼" galvanized steel
    C. ¼" copper tubing   D. High-strength PVC plastic

9. The horizontal band of material directly beneath a   9.___
    cornice, and above the siding, is known as the
    A. gable   B. section   C. perimeter   D. frieze

10. Approximately how many hours are typically required for   10.___
    carpenter labor to install 1,000 square feet of plywood
    floor sheathing?
    A. 1-3   B. 3-4   C. 5-6   D. 7-8

11. The generally accepted method for figuring *in-place* costs 11.___
    for small accessories such as doorbells, smoke alarms,
    and garage door openers is to multiply the material cost
    by
        A. ½   B. 2   C. 3   D. 4

12. A _____ is represented by the mechanical symbol 12.___
    shown at the right.
        A. diaphragm valve   B. lock and shield valve
        C. gate valve   D. check valve

13. What is used to join lengths of galvanized steel pipe? 13.___
        A. Molten solder   B. Threaded ends and sealer
        C. Elbows   D. Lead-and-oakum seal

14. Approximately how much plumber's labor would be required 14.___
    for the installation of a single chrome-plated faucet set?
        A. 15 minutes   B. 30 minutes
        C. 1 hour   D. 1½ hours

15. Each of the following roof flashing materials takes about 15.___
    the same amount of time to install EXCEPT
        A. aluminum   B. galvanized steel
        C. zinc alloy   D. stainless steel

16. What is the MOST commonly used grade of asphalt tile used 16.___
    for resilient flooring?
        A. A   B. B   C. C   D. D

17. Which of the following plastic pipe materials is usable 17.___
    for hot water lines?
        A. DWV   B. ABS   C. PVC   D. PVDC

18. Approximately how many linear feet of gutter material 18.___
    can be installed by one person in an average work day?
        A. 80   B. 120   C. 150   D. 175

19. What is represented by the electrical symbol 19.___
    shown at the right?
        A. Junction box   B. Blanked outlet
        C. Television outlet   D. Buzzer

20. When estimating the cost of resilient flooring material, 20.___
    how much floor tile and base should be calculated as
    waste?
        A. 5%   B. 10%   C. 20%   D. 30%

21. Most fire codes suggest that wall surfaces within _____ 21.___
    of a fireplace unit be covered with a fire-retardant
    surface.
        A. 8 inches   B. 16 inches   C. 4 feet   D. 8 feet

22. Wood, gypsum board, or expanded metal used as a base   22.____
    for plaster finish is known as
       A. parging   B. lath   C. chord   D. aggregate

23. Approximately how many linear feet of sewer pipe can be   23.____
    installed in an average work day?
       A. 25   B. 50   C. 75   D. 100

24. Approximately how many square feet of board floor   24.____
    sheathing can be installed by a crew in a normal work day?
       A. 250   B. 500   C. 750   D. 1,000

25. A _____ line is represented by the mechanical   _ _ _ _   25.____
    symbol shown at the right.
       A. soil   B. refrigerant
       C. cold water   D. hot water

———

KEY (CORRECT ANSWERS)

1. C		11. B	
2. C		12. A	
3. C		13. B	
4. B		14. C	
5. B		15. A	
6. A		16. C	
7. B		17. D	
8. A		18. B	
9. D		19. D	
10. D		20. B	

21. A
22. B
23. B
24. C
25. D

———

TEST 3

DIRECTIONS: Each question or incomplete statement is followed by several suggested answers or completions. Select the one that BEST answers the question or completes the statement. *PRINT THE LETTER OF THE CORRECT ANSWER IN THE SPACE AT THE RIGHT.*

1. Which of the following plumbing (pipe) materials would be LEAST expensive to install?   1.___
   A. ¼" galvanized steel   B. 1" copper pipe
   C. ¼" copper tubing   D. High-strength PVC plastic

2. Which of the following roof flashing materials would take the GREATEST amount of time to install?   2.___
   A. Aluminum   B. Stainless steel
   C. Zinc alloy   D. Copper

3. Approximately how many square feet of *Venetian* blind window accessory can be installed by a worker in an average day?   3.___
   A. 50   B. 100   C. 225   D. 450

4. What is the term for a short length of pipe threaded at each end and used to connect fittings?   4.___
   A. Joist   B. Nipple   C. ABS   D. Elbow

5. Approximately how many square yards of metal lathing work can be installed for a ceiling in a typical work day?   5.___
   A. 30-40   B. 50-60   C. 60-80   D. 85-100

6. The approximate weight specification for a 20-year bonded flat roof is _____ pounds per square foot of roof area.   6.___
   A. 3   B. 6   C. 9   D. 12

7. Approximately how many linear feet of PVC pipe can be installed in a typical work day?   7.___
   A. 35-40   B. 50-60   C. 65-75   D. 85-100

8. Each of the following is a primary factor in the pricing of finishing hardware EXCEPT   8.___
   A. finish   B. size   C. quality   D. use

9. What is the nominal length, in inches, of most ordered studs?   9.___
   A. 48   B. 60   C. 72   D. 96

10. The bottom member of a window assembly, which forms the sill, is the   10.___
    A. stringer   B. riser   C. slump   D. stool

11. For how many hours should a *D label* fire door be able to   11.___
    withstand continuous fire exposure?
       A. 3/4   B. 1   C. 1½   D. 3

12. What type of window frame is anodized?   12.___
       A. Steel   B. Aluminum   C. Bronze   D. Wood

13. On average, the cost of materials for a job will be   13.___
    about _____% of the total job cost.
       A. 15   B. 35   C. 55   D. 85

14. Each of the following means is used to secure vertical   14.___
    metal studs to wall plates EXCEPT
       A. sheet metal screws   B. spot welding
       C. tie wire   D. soldering

15. How much time should be estimated for the installation   15.___
    of a fire door and frame?
       A. 30 minutes   B. 1 hour
       C. 2 hours   D. 4 hours

16. Which of the following would NOT be a color of grade A   16.___
    asphalt tile?
       A. Black   B. Green   C. Yellow   D. Brown

17. Concrete for on-grade floor installations should typically   17.___
    have an aggregate size of not more than _____ inch.
       A. ¼   B. ½   C. 3/4   D. 1

18. Which type of estimate is MOST often used with change   18.___
    orders?
       A. Quantity survey
       B. Lump-sum amount
       C. Cost-per-square-foot estimate
       D. Unit cost estimate

19. Which of the following types of glass will be LEAST   19.___
    expensive?
       A. Grade B sheet
       B. ¼" wire glass
       C. Mirror
       D. 1/8" patterned *obscure* glass

20. According to established finish-designation standards,   20.___
    which of the following finish materials would be ranked
    at the HIGHEST grade?
       A. Chromium-plated   B. Bright bronze
       C. Stainless steel   D. Lacquered satin aluminum

21. What is represented by the mechanical symbol   21.___
    shown at the right?
       A. Door   B. Scale trap
       C. Strainer   D. T connection

22. Most metal roofs require a waterproof underlayment that weighs about _____ pounds per 100 square feet of roof area.

    A. 30   B. 60   C. 100   D. 125

22.___

23. A material used over a rough subfloor that will provide a smooth surface for the finish floor is termed a(n)

    A. soffit   B. underlayment
    C. vapor barrier   D. molding

23.___

24. Approximately how many square feet of wood strip flooring can be installed in one hour?

    A. 50   B. 125   C. 225   D. 300

24.___

25. The scale of a typical site plans uses $\frac{1}{4}$" to represent

    A. 1 inch   B. 1 foot   C. 25 feet   D. 100 feet

25.___

KEY (CORRECT ANSWERS)

1. C		11. C	
2. D		12. B	
3. D		13. D	
4. B		14. D	
5. C		15. B	
6. B		16. C	
7. A		17. C	
8. B		18. B	
9. D		19. A	
10. D		20. C	

21. C
22. A
23. B
24. D
25. D

EXAMINATION SECTION
TEST 1

DIRECTIONS: Each question or incomplete statement is followed by several suggested answers or completions. Select the one that BEST answers the question or completes the statement. *PRINT THE LETTER OF THE CORRECT ANSWER IN THE SPACE AT THE RIGHT.*

1. An unbalanced bid is a bidding device used by the contractor. An example of unbalanced bidding is to put   1.___
   A. lower unit prices in all unit price items to submit a low bid
   B. lower prices on lump sum items and higher prices on unit price items
   C. lower unit prices on secondary items and higher unit prices on primary items
   D. higher prices on items built early and lower prices on items built later

2. Clearing and grubbing as related to excavation mean cutting trees   2.___
   A. so that 1 foot remains above ground
   B. so that 6 inches remains above ground
   C. to ground level
   D. and removing the stumps of the trees

3. The size of a bulldozer is measured by its   3.___
   A. weight   B. flywheel horsepower
   C. ripping capacity   D. coefficient of traction

4. Of the following, an important use of geotextiles is   4.___
   A. as a filter in drainage control
   B. to improve the density of soil
   C. to increase the plasticity of soil
   D. to reduce the CBR of soil

5. A graphical procedure employing a control chart is sometimes used for statistical control in highway construction. After charts of individual tests are prepared, the upper and lower limits are usually _____ standard deviation(s) from a central value.   5.___
   A. one   B. two   C. three   D. four

6. On a highway construction job, slope stakes are usually set on both sides of the road at intervals of _____ feet.   6.___
   A. 25   B. 50   C. 75   D. 100

7. Earth grade stakes are usually set   7.___
   A. when the slope stakes are set
   B. at the center line of the road
   C. after final grading is completed
   D. after rough grading operations have been completed

8. In a borrow pit, measurements for the volume of earth removed are taken usually at _____ foot intervals.
    A. 25   B. 50   C. 75   D. 100

8.___

9. In placing surveying stakes for a culvert, a stake is set at the center line of the culvert. A horizontal line on the stake gives the amount of cut or fill to the _____ of the culvert.
    A. top   B. center   C. flow line D. subgrade

9.___

10. Aeolian soils are soils formed by
    A. glacial action   B. volcanic action
    C. being carried by water D. being carried by wind

10.___

11. Specific gravity of soils are in the range of
    A. 2.3 to 2.5   B. 2.4 to 2.6
    C. 2.5 to 2.7   D. 2.6 to 2.8

11.___

12. Of the following soils, the one that is most highly compressible has a _____ plastic limit and _____ liquid limit.
    A. low; high   B. low; low
    C. high; low   D. high; high

12.___

13. In the present ASSHTO soil classification systems, soils are classified into groups. The number of basic groups are
    A. 6   B. 7   C. 8   D. 9

13.___

14. In the present AASHTO soil classification system, granular materials are primarily in Group(s)
    A. A1 *only*   B. A1 and A2
    C. A1, A2, and A3   D. A1, A2, A3, and A4

14.___

15. The optimum moisture content of a soil occurs when under a given compactive effort, the soil has a maximum
    A. void ratio   B. plasticity index
    C. elasticity   D. density

15.___

16. The liquid limit that separates an A4 soil from an A5 soil is
    A. 10   B. 20   C. 30   D. 40

16.___

17. As part of the soil classification in a given soil is an abbreviation NP. This is an abbreviation for no
    A. permeability
    B. plasticity
    C. peat or other organic materials
    D. porosity

17.___

18. For granular materials, the maximum allowable percent passing a Number 200 sieve is
    A. 20   B. 25   C. 30   D. 35

18.___

19.

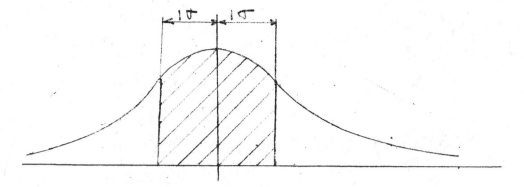

In the normal or Gauss distribution shown above, the shaded area is one standard deviation on either side of the central value covering _____ of the area under the curve.
    A. 60%   B. 62%   C. 65%   D. 68%

Questions 20-25.

DIRECTIONS: Questions 20 through 25, inclusive, refer to the diagram below of a vertical curve.

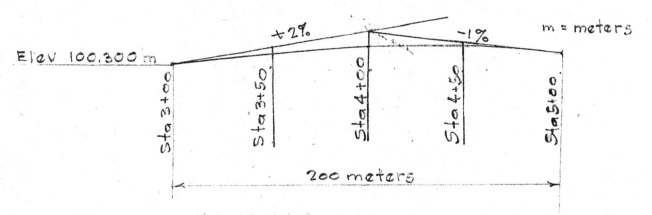

20.   The elevation of the curve at Sta4+00 is _____ meters.   20.___
      A. 101.250   B. 101.350   C. 101.850   D. 102.150

21.   The grade of the curve at Sta4+00 is   21.___
      A. +.5%   B. +.75%   C. +1.00%   D. +1.25%

22.   The elevation of the curve at Sta3+50 is _____ meters.   22.___
      A. 100.992   B. 101.012   C. 101.112   D. 101.212

23.   The grade of the curve at Sta3+50 is   23.___
      A. 1.75%   B. 1.50%   C. 1.38%   D. 1.25%

24.   The station of the high point is   24.___
      A. 4+08.333   B. 4+16.667   C. 4+25.000   D. 4+33.333

25.   The elevation of the high point is _____ meters.   25.___
      A. 101.633   B. 101.750   C. 101.833   D. 101.917

KEY (CORRECT ANSWERS)

1. D		11. D	
2. D		12. A	
3. B		13. B	
4. A		14. C	
5. C		15. D	
6. B		16. D	
7. D		17. B	
8. A		18. D	
9. C		19. D	
10. D		20. B	

21. A
22. C
23. D
24. D
25. A

TEST 2

DIRECTIONS: Each question or incomplete statement is followed by several suggested answers or completions. Select the one that BEST answers the question or completes the statement. *PRINT THE LETTER OF THE CORRECT ANSWER IN THE SPACE AT THE RIGHT.*

Questions 1-3.

DIRECTIONS: Questions 1 through 3 refer to the diagram below.

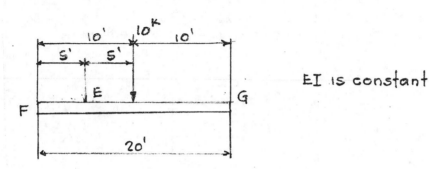

EI is constant

1. The deflection at the center of the beam is   1.___

  A. $-\dfrac{1670^{k13}}{EI}$ B. $-\dfrac{2000^{k13}}{EI}$ C. $-\dfrac{2330^{k13}}{EI}$ D. $-\dfrac{2670^{k13}}{EI}$

2. The slope at F is   2.___

  A. $-\dfrac{200^{k12}}{EI}$ B. $-\dfrac{225^{k12}}{EI}$ C. $-\dfrac{250^{k12}}{EI}$ D. $-\dfrac{275^{k12}}{EI}$

3. The deflection at E is   3.___

  A. $-\dfrac{996^{k13}}{EI}$ B. $-\dfrac{1046^{k13}}{EI}$ C. $-\dfrac{1096^{k13}}{EI}$ D. $-\dfrac{1146^{k13}}{EI}$

Questions 4-7.

DIRECTIONS: Questions 4 through 7, inclusive, refer to the truss below.

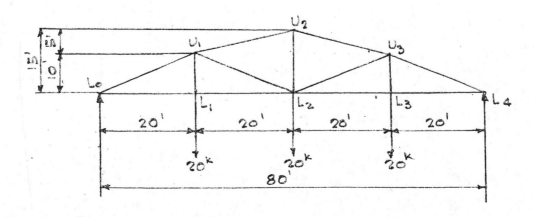

4. The load in member L_1-L_2 is   4.____
   A. $+30^k$ B. $+40^k$ C. $+50^k$ D. $+60^k$

5. The load in member U_1-U_2 is   5.____
   A. -50.9^k B. -52.9^k C. -54.9^k D. -56.9^k

6. The load in member U_1-L_2 is   6.____
   A. -3.4^k B. -5.4^k C. -7.4^k D. -9.4^k

7. The load in member U_2-L_2 is   7.____
   A. $+24.6^k$ B. $+26.6^k$ C. $+28.6^k$ D. $+30.6^k$

Questions 8-11.

DIRECTIONS: Questions 8 through 11, inclusive, refer to the diagram below of a beam with fixed ends.

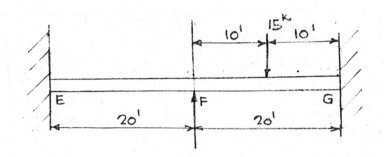

8. The moment in E is   8.____
   A. 9.4^{1k} B. 12.6^{1k} C. 14.8^{1k} D. 17.0^{1k}

9. The moment in G is   9.____
   A. 37.5^{1k} B. 40.0^{1k} C. 43.0^{1k} D. 46.9^{1k}

10. The moment at F is   10.____
   A. 14.4^{1k} B. 18.8^{1k} C. 23.2^{1k} D. 27.6^{1k}

11. The vertical reaction at E is   11.____
   A. -0.4^k B. -1.4^k C. -2.4^k D. -3.4^k

12. The former First Lady of the United States who had   12.____
legislation enacted to plant wild flowers adjacent to
federal highways is
   A. Rosalyn Carter   B. Barbara Bush
   C. Jackie Kennedy   D. Lady Bird Johnson

13. *Scarification* as used in the specifications means   13.____
   A. removing rust from a surface
   B. removing paint from a surface
   C. cleaning equipment
   D. loosening topsoil

14. A proposal by the contractor producing a savings to the
    department without impairing essential functions and
    characteristics of the facility is termed a(n)
    A. alternative suggestion
    B. design efficiency proposal
    C. value engineering proposal
    D. force account economy

14.___

15. A cubic meter is MOST NEARLY equal to _____ cubic yards.
    A. 1.31   B. 1.33   C. 1.35   D. 1.37

15.___

16. One hectare is equal to MOST NEARLY _____ acres.
    A. 2   B. 2.5   C. 3.0   D. 3.5

16.___

17. One newton is MOST NEARLY equal to _____ pounds.
    A. .12   B. .17   C. .22   D. .29

17.___

18. A metric ton is _____ pounds.
    A. 2200   B. 2400   C. 2600   D. 2800

18.___

19. A piezometer is a device that measures
    A. hydraulic pressure   B. soil compaction
    C. soil grain size   D. soil grain strength

19.___

20. Portland cement type 2 is _____ cement.
    A. high early strength
    B. low heat
    C. air entraining
    D. moderate sulfate resisting

20.___

21. Wire shall have a minimum yield strength of 240 MPa.
    The MPa is an abbreviation of _____ pascals.
    A. macro   B. micro   C. milli   D. mega

21.___

22. 7°C is, in degrees Fahrenheit,
    A. 42.6   B. 44.6   C. 46.6   D. 48.6

22.___

23. In a concrete mix, the absolute ratio of the weight of
    water to the weight of cement is .44. If a bag of cement
    weighs 94 pounds and there are 7.48 gallons in a cubic
    foot, the number of gallons of water per bag of cement
    for this ratio is MOST NEARLY
    A. 5.0   B. 5.5   C. 5.8   D. 6.1

23.___

24. The specifications require that when transit mixed
    concrete is used, approximately 90% of the design water
    is added followed by mixing the concrete in the drum of
    the truck. The remainder of the design water may be
    added
    A. after half the load is emptied
    B. to meet the water cement ratio requirement
    C. if the mix is not uniform
    D. to attain a suitable slump

24.___

25. For highways, the minimum median width in a divided   25.___
    highway is _____ feet.
    A. 2   B. 3   C. 4   D. 5

———

KEY (CORRECT ANSWERS)

1. A		11. B	
2. C		12. D	
3. D		13. D	
4. D		14. C	
5. C		15. A	
6. C		16. B	
7. B		17. C	
8. A		18. A	
9. D		19. A	
10. B		20. D	

21. D
22. B
23. A
24. D
25. C

———

EXAMINATION SECTION
TEST 1

DIRECTIONS: Each question or incomplete statement is followed by several suggested answers or completions. Select the one that BEST answers the question or completes the statement. *PRINT THE LETTER OF THE CORRECT ANSWER IN THE SPACE AT THE RIGHT.*

1. Reinforcing steel is coated with epoxy primarily to _____ of the steel.
   A. prevent corrosion
   B. improve the electric conductivity
   C. increase the tensile strength
   D. increase the compressive strength

   1.___

2. Specifications for concrete require that concrete shall reach or exceed the design strength at the end of _____ days.
   A. 14   B. 21   C. 28   D. 35

   2.___

3. A #6 reinforcing bar has a cross-section area of _____ square inches.
   A. .44   B. .48   C. .52   D. .56

   3.___

4. Mixing time for concrete which is measured from the time all ingredients are in the drum should be at least 1.5 minutes for a one cubic yard mixer plus 0.5 minutes for each cubic yard of capacity over one cubic yard.
   The MINIMUM time to mix 7 cubic yards of concrete is, in minutes,
   A. 3.0   B. 3.5   C. 4.0   D. 4.5

   4.___

5. It is recommended that a maximum limit be set on mixing time for machine-mixed concrete because overmixing may remove entrained air and
   A. increase the water/cement ratio of the mixture
   B. increase the amount of fine aggregates in the concrete mixture
   C. the concrete mix may set prematurely
   D. cause excess water to rise in the placed concrete causing alligator cracks in the surface

   5.___

6.

   6.___

   Of the following curves, the shape of the roadway section shown above is
   A. circular   B. elliptical C. parabolic D. hyperbolic

7.

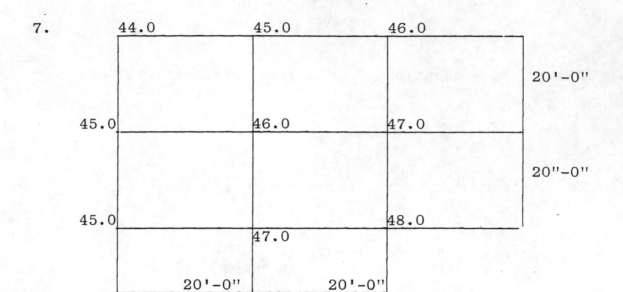

44.0	45.0	46.0

Shown above are the elevations of a borrow pit. The final elevation of the borrow pit after removing the soil is 40.0. Neglecting earth removal outside the borrow pit area, the volume of earth removed is, in cubic yards, MOST NEARLY

A. 347   B. 352   C. 357   D. 362

8. The shaded area is, in square inches, MOST NEARLY
   A. 18.3
   B. 19.1
   C. 20.0
   D. 20.9

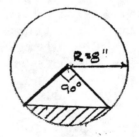

9. Of the following properties of polymer concrete that make it attractive for maintenance of Portland cement concrete roadways, the one that is MOST important is
   A. light weight
   B. immunity to corrosion
   C. resistance to abrasion
   D. rapid hardening qualities

10. A gallon of water weighs MOST NEARLY _____ pounds.
    A. 7.53   B. 8.33   C. 9.13   D. 9.53

7.___

8.___

9.___

10.___

11. Air-entrained concrete is used in concrete roadways   11._____
    primarily to
    A. reduce the weight of the concrete
    B. prevent corrosion of the steel reinforcement in
       the concrete
    C. make the concrete less porous to the intrusion of
       water in the concrete
    D. resist damage to the roadway due to freezing and
       thawing

12. The slump test in concrete is used to test its   12._____
    A. air content   B. workability
    C. porosity   D. uniformity

13. The criterion for water that is to be used for mixing   13._____
    concrete is that it should be potable. This means that
    the water should
    A. have high turbidity
    B. should be hard
    C. contain no sulfates
    D. be fit for human consumption

14. A test that can be used on an asphalt roadway to measure   14._____
    changes in hardness due to age hardening is a _____ test.
    A. ductility
    B. viscosity
    C. ring and ball softening point
    D. penetration

15. A densely graded bituminous mixture is called a large   15._____
    stone mix if the nominal size of aggregates is equal
    to or greater than a minimum of
    A. 1 inch   B. 1¼ inches C. 1½ inches D. 1 3/4 inches

16. The specifications state that the surface on which the   16._____
    bituminous material is applied must have a temperature
    of 20°C or higher.
    20°C is, in degrees Fahrenheit,
    A. 62°   B. 64°   C. 66°   D. 68°

17. The largest size aggregate in sheet asphalt is usually   17._____
    A. 1/8 inch   B. 1/4 inch   C. 3/8 inch   D. 1/2 inch

18. Sheet asphalt is used mainly in   18._____
    A. rural areas   B. major highways
    C. overpasses   D. city streets

19. Of the following, a slurry seal is NOT used on a   19._____
    bituminous pavement to
    A. fill potholes
    B. fill cracks
    C. repair raveling asphalt pavement
    D. provide a skid-resistant surface

20. Pozzolan is a *siliceous* material. Another example of a siliceous material is
    A. clay   B. limestone C. granite   D. sand

21. The primary purpose of a tack coat that precedes the application of a bitumimous mix on an existing surface is to
    A. remove dust from the existing surface
    B. fill in cracks in the existing surface
    C. allow the new mixture to adhere to the existing surface
    D. prevent the asphalt in the bituminous paving material from seeping into the existing pavement

22. The lowest temperature at which asphalt pavements should be laid is
    A. 30°F   B. 40°F   C. 50°F   D. 60°F

23. Steam will rise from an asphalt mix when it is dumped into the hopper of a paver if
    A. there is too little asphalt in the mix
    B. excess moisture is present in the mix
    C. the mix is too hot
    D. there is an excess of asphalt in the mix

24. The number of millimeters in an inch is MOST NEARLY
    A. 20   B. 25   C. 30   D. 35

25. The number of inches in a meter is MOST NEARLY
    A. 39.37   B. 39.57   C. 39.77   D. 39.97

KEY (CORRECT ANSWERS)

1. A		11. D
2. C		12. B
3. A		13. D
4. D		14. D
5. B		15. A
6. C		16. D
7. B		17. B
8. A		18. D
9. D		19. A
10. B		20. D
	21. C	
	22. B	
	23. B	
	24. B	
	25. A	

TEST 2

DIRECTIONS: Each question or incomplete statement is followed by several suggested answers or completions. Select the one that BEST answers the question or completes the statement. *PRINT THE LETTER OF THE CORRECT ANSWER IN THE SPACE AT THE RIGHT.*

1. Overheated asphalt can often be identified from the _____ in the truck.   1.___
   A. rich black appearance and the tendency to slump
   B. slump and leveling out
   C. blue smoke rising from the mix
   D. lean, granular appearance of the mix

2. Of the following, the traffic sign shown at the right indicates a   2.___
   A. school crossing
   B. no passing zone
   C. railroad crossing
   D. deer crossing

3. 90 kilometers per hour is MOST NEARLY _____ miles per hour.   3.___
   A. 40   B. 45   C. 50   D. 55

4. One kilometer is equal to _____ miles.   4.___
   A. 0.5   B. 0.6   C. 0.7   D. 0.8

5. Steel weighs 490 pounds per cubic foot. A one inch square bar of steel one foot long weighs MOST NEARLY _____ pounds.   5.___
   A. 3.0   B. 3.4   C. 3.8   D. 4.2

6. The size of the fillet weld is dimension   6.___
   A. A
   B. B
   C. C
   D. D

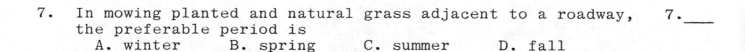

7. In mowing planted and natural grass adjacent to a roadway, the preferable period is   7.___
   A. winter   B. spring   C. summer   D. fall

8. Pumping of a roadway surface occurs on
    A. bituminous pavements only
    B. bituminous and concrete pavements
    C. concrete pavements only
    D. concrete pavements only if they are not air-entrained

9. Pumping of a roadway surface is associated with soils in the subgrade that are
    A. gravelly
    B. fine grained
    C. coarse grained
    D. distributed in size from fine grained soils to coarse grained soils

10. The buckling or blowup of old concrete pavements is due primarily to the
    A. failure of longitudinal and transverse joints to function properly
    B. pounding by trucks that the pavement was not designed to carry
    C. failure of the subgrade to transfer the loads upon it
    D. subsurface water that is not drained from beneath the pavement

11. The MOST common type of construction equipment used for clearing and grubbing activities is a bulldozer. Bulldozer size is determined by
    A. tread area   B. blade size
    C. drawbar pull   D. flywheel horsepower

12. Sheepsfoot rollers are BEST used to compact
    A. clay soils
    B. sandy soils
    C. gravelly soils
    D. graded sand and gravel mix

13. A smooth-wheeled steel roller that is typically water ballasted are most effective on
    A. granular material such as sand and gravel
    B. clayed material
    C. mixtures of silt, sand and clay
    D. mixtures of sand and clay

14. Of the following machines, the one that would be MOST suitable for grading and shaping surfaces, ditching and bank sloping would be a
    A. bulldozer   B. motor grader
    C. front end loader   D. backhoe

15. Supercompactors which are useful for all types of soils weigh from _____ tons.
    A. 10 to 40   B. 20 to 50   C. 30 to 60   D. 40 to 70

16. A basic objective of the Critical Path Method used on a   16.____
    highway construction project would be to
    A. achieve economies in the use of material
    B. achieve economies in the use of equipment
    C. improve the quality of construction
    D. prevent the creation of bottlenecks

17. In the Critical Path Method, free float is the amount   17.____
    of time
    A. an activity requires to be completed
    B. an activity can be delayed without causing a delay
       in the succeeding activity
    C. an activity takes to make up for the time lag in
       the following activity
    D. needed to make up for lost time in a preceding
       activity

18. Another name for the bar chart used in construction   18.____
    planning and scheduling is the _____ chart.
    A. Fischer   B. Schiff   C. Banff   D. Gantt

19. Of the following, the machine that would LEAST likely   19.____
    be used to excavate large volumes of earth is a
    A. scraper   B. front end loader
    C. shovel   D. clamshell

20. Roadside maintenance generally includes the area between   20.____
    the
    A. traveled surface and the limits of the right of way
    B. distance between the outer edges of the shoulders
       on opposite sides of the highway
    C. median strip of the highway
    D. distance between the right of way on opposite sides
       of the highway

21. The sewer that usually has the greatest depth below grade   21.____
    is usually a(n) _____ sewer.
    A. sanitary   B. combined
    C. intercepting   D. relieving

22. A combined sewer is a sewer that   22.____
    A. carries storm water and salty water
    B. is made of steel and lined on the inside with
       concrete
    C. sometimes flow less than full and sometimes is
       under pressure
    D. carries sewage and storm water

23. If the grade of a sewer is 0.5%, the change in the   23.____
    elevation of the invert of the sewer in 350 feet is, in
    feet and inches,
    A. 1'-9"   B. 1'-10"   C. 1'-11"   D. 2'-0"

24. The National Joint Committee has adopted a color code
     for traffic control devices. The color brown is used
     for
         A. direction guidance
         B. general warning
         C. motorist service guidance
         D. public recreation and scenic guidance

25. Of the following, the isosceles traffic
     sign shown at the right indicates a
         A. traffic separation
         B. no U turn
         C. narrow median-urban
         D. no passing zone

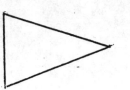

KEY (CORRECT ANSWERS)

1. C		11. D	
2. A		12. A	
3. D		13. A	
4. B		14. B	
5. B		15. B	
6. A		16. D	
7. D		17. B	
8. C		18. D	
9. B		19. D	
10. A		20. A	

21. C
22. D
23. A
24. D
25. D

EXAMINATION SECTION
TEST 1

DIRECTIONS: Each question or incomplete statement is followed by several suggested answers or completions. Select the one that BEST answers the question or completes the statement. *PRINT THE LETTER OF THE CORRECT ANSWER IN THE SPACE AT THE RIGHT.*

1. Reflective cracks in asphalt overlays   1.___
   A. are cracks in asphalt overlays that show the crack pattern of the pavement underneath
   B. are cracks that reflect caused by weakness in the base soil
   C. are the result of change in weights and frequency of truck travel in that they are greater than the loads the pavement was designed for
   D. reflect the type of cracks that normally could be expected for this type of pavement

2. In a guide for the estimation of Pavement Condition Rating   2.___
   for asphalt concrete pavement on a highway is the following classification: *Pavement is in fairly good condition with frequent slight cracking or very slight channeling and a few areas with slight alligatoring. Rideability is fairly good with intermittent rough and uneven sections.*
   The maintenance recommendation for this class of pavement condition is
   A. no maintenance required
   B. normal maintenance only
   C. resurface in 3 to 5 years
   D. resurface within 3 years

3. A major problem in bituminous asphalt plants is   3.___
   A. varying water content in the bituminous aggregate
   B. accuracy in the weighing equipment
   C. air pollution caused by plant exhausts
   D. producing a uniform mixture

4. The primary difference between asphalt concrete and sheet   4.___
   asphalt is asphalt concrete
   A. uses a finer sand than sheet asphalt
   B. uses a lower viscosity asphalt than sheet asphalt
   C. generally has a thinner layer than sheet asphalt
   D. contains coarse aggregate whereas sheet asphalt does not have coarse aggregate

5. It is common practice to apply a prime coat over untreated   5.___
   and some treated bases before asphalt concrete is placed. Of the following, the reasons for applying a prime coat are to

    A. bind loose particles of the base and minimize heat loss in the applied asphalt concrete
    B. act as a bond between base and pavement and prevent loss of asphalt in the asphalt concrete due to seepage
    C. deter rising moisture from penetrating the pavement and minimize heat loss in the applied asphalt concrete
    D. bind loose particles in the base and deter rising moisture from penetrating the asphalt pavement

6. The asphalt content of open graded mixes is generally at   6.___
    A. the same level as dense graded asphalt
    B. a higher level than dense graded asphalt
    C. a lower level than dense graded asphalt
    D. at a higher or lower level than dense graded asphalt depending on the percent of fine aggregate in the open graded asphalt mix

7. Sheet asphalt was extensively used in the past with a   7.___
thickness of _____ inch(es).
    A. 1/2   B. 3/4   C. 1   D. 1½

8. The progressive separation of aggregate particles in a   8.___
pavement from the surface downward or from the edges inward in an asphalt concrete pavement is known as
    A. raveling   B. spalling
    C. scaling   D. reflective cracks

9. A profilometer used on an asphalt concrete road measures   9.___
the _____ the road.
    A. grade of   B. roughness of
    C. impact resistance of   D. channels in

10. Reinforcing steel is used in a footing. The minimum   10.___
distance the bottom of the steel is above the subgrade should be _____ inch(es).
    A. 1   B. 2   C. 3   D. 4

11. Loose sand weighs 120 pounds per cubic foot and the   11.___
specific gravity of sand is 2.65. The absolute volume of a cubic foot of loose sand is, in cubic feet, most nearly
    A. .73   B. .75   C. .77   D. .79

12. The maximum size of coarse aggregate in a concrete mix   12.___
for a reinforced concrete structure is determined by the size of the concrete section and the
    A. type of cement used
    B. proportion of fine aggregate
    C. minimum distance between reinforcing bars
    D. yield point of the reinforcing steel

13. Cement (High Early Strength) is Type _____ cement.   13.___
    A. I   B. II   C. III   D. IV

14. Slump in concrete is a measure of   14.___
    A. strength   B. porosity
    C. permeability   D. workability

15. The cross section area of a #8 bar is _____ square inches.   15.___
    A. .60   B. .79   C. 1.00   D. 1.25

16. Construction joints for slabs in a building shall be made   16.___
    A. at the supports
    B. within 1/8 of the span of the slab from the supports
    C. from 1/8 to 3/8 of the span of the slab from the
       supports
    D. near the center of the span

17. Chutes for depositing concrete shall have a slope no   17.___
greater than
    A.   B.   C.   D.

18. Air entrained cement is used in a concrete mix on   18.___
highways primarily to
    A. make the concrete stronger after 28 days
    B. have a higher early strength
    C. make the surface more resistant to freezing and
       thawing
    D. make the surface less porous to better resist the
       impact of trucks

19. Beach sand is unsuitable as a fine aggregate in concrete   19.___
because it has salt contamination and the sand particles
are
    A. smooth   B. rough
    C. uniform in size   D. too fine

20. The fineness modulus of sand for concrete is taken on   20.___
the job to insure
    A. the quality of the sand
    B. that the gradation of the sand does not change
    C. that there is not an excess of fines in the sand
    D. that there is not an excess of oversized particles
       in the sand

21. The coarse and fine aggregate for concrete are usually   21.___
tested
    A. at the quarry site
    B. at the job site
    C. by sampling a loaded truck
    D. in the design engineering office

22. The slump in concrete for highway mixtures range from _____ inches.   22. __
    A. 1 to 3   B. 2 to 5   C. 3 to 6   D. 4 to 7

23. A bag of cement weighs _____ pounds.   23. __
    A. 90   B. 94   C. 97   D. 100

24. The design strength of concrete is to be reached at the end of _____ days.   24. __
    A. 7   B. 14   C. 21   D. 28

25. Of the following, water-cement ratio may be defined as _____ of water per _____ of cement.   25. __
    A. gallons; bag   B. gallons; 100 pounds
    C. quarts; bag   D. quarts; 100 pounds

_____

KEY (CORRECT ANSWERS)

1. A		11. A
2. C		12. C
3. C		13. C
4. D		14. D
5. D		15. B
6. B		16. D
7. D		17. C
8. A		18. C
9. B		19. C
10. C		20. B

21. A
22. A
23. B
24. D
25. A

_____

TEST 2

DIRECTIONS: Each question or incomplete statement is followed by several suggested answers or completions. Select the one that BEST answers the question or completes the statement. *PRINT THE LETTER OF THE CORRECT ANSWER IN THE SPACE AT THE RIGHT.*

1. The maximum size of coarse aggregate in a concrete mix for a reinforced concrete structure is determined by the size of the section and the
   A. type of cement used
   B. proportion of fine aggregate
   C. minimum distance between reinforcing bars
   D. the yield point of the reinforcing steel

1.___

Questions 2-3.

DIRECTIONS: Questions 2 and 3 refer to concrete mix design.

2. The present and most popular method of rational mixture design is sponsored by ACI committee 211, 1994. In this method, the design using ordinary cement is based on
   A. slump and water-cement ratio
   B. aggregate size and water-cement ratio
   C. slump, aggregate size, and water-cement ratio
   D. slump and water content

2.___

3. In the method of mix design of ACI committee 211, 1994, water content is expressed in
   A. pounds of water per bag of cement
   B. pounds of water per cubic foot of concrete
   C. gallons of water per cubic yard of concrete
   D. pounds of water per cubic yard of concrete

3.___

4. The right to use or control the property of another for designated purposes is the definition of
   A. property acquisition   B. right-of-way
   C. an air right   D. an easement

4.___

5. A 24 inch circular drainage pipe is shown on a profile drawing of a highway as an ellipse with the major axis vertical. The reason for this is
   A. the horizontal and vertical scales of the profile drawing are different
   B. the pipe is not perpendicular to the center line of the roadway
   C. to emphasize the height of the pipe
   D. the slope of the pipe is taken into account

5.___

6. On a highway plan is a note for #4 wire game fence
   reading Lt Sta 2970 + 00 to 2979 + 85, Rt Sta 2970 + 00
   to 2980 + 70. The total number of linear feet of new
   #4 wire game fence is, in feet, most nearly
     A. 1955   B. 2005   C. 2055   D. 2105

   6.___

7. The superelevation of a curve is .075 feet. The superelevation, in inches, is most nearly
     A. 9   B. 5/8   C. 3/4   D. 7/8

   7.___

8. On a plan for a highway is a note $\dfrac{S.C.}{Sta\ 2968+56.50}$. The
   S.C. is an abbreviation for
     A. slope at curve   B. spiral to circular curve
     C. superelevated curve   D. separation at center

   8.___

9. Of the following methods of soil stabilization for the
   base of a highway pavement, the one that is most effective
   is
     A. a cement admixture
     B. a lime admixture
     C. an emulsified asphalt treated soil
     D. mechanical soil stabilization

   9.___

10. An asphalt pavement mixture having a brownish dull appear-
    ance and lacking a shiny black luster
      A. is normal for an asphalt mixture
      B. contains too little aggregate
      C. is too cold
      D. contains too little asphalt

    10.___

11. Steam rising from an asphalt mix when it is dumped into
    a hopper indicates
      A. there is excessive moisture in the aggregate
      B. the mix is overheated
      C. emulsification is taking place
      D. the mixture has not been adequately mixed

    11.___

12. The disadvantage of excessive fine aggregate in an asphalt
    mix is
      A. it is difficult to get a uniform mix
      B. it will require an excessive amount of asphalt
      C. it is difficult to apply because of the grittiness
        of the mix
      D. the final surface will tend to be rough

    12.___

13. On highways where heavy trucks are permitted, the percent
    of total traffic that are heavy trucks is, in percent,
    MOST NEARLY
      A. 4   B. 11   C. 18   D. 25

    13.___

14. A single axle 80 kN load is equal to _____ pounds per axle.
      A. 12,000   B. 14,000   C. 16,000   D. 18,000

    14.___

15. Normal traffic growth in the United States is _____   15.___
    percent per year.
    A. 1-2   B. 3-5   C. 5-7   D. 7-9

16. EAL is an abbreviation for _____ axle load   16.___
    A. equal   B. equivalent
    C. effective   D. estimated

17. A roughometer is a single-wheeled trailer instrumented   17.___
    to measure the roughness of a pavement surface. The
    measure is in inches per
    A. foot   B. yard
    C. hundred yards   D. mile

18. The Atterberg Limit is a test on   18.___
    A. coarse aggregate   B. asphalt
    C. soil   D. Portland cement

19. Of the following, the one that is a high strength bolt   19.___
    is designated
    A. A7   B. A36   C. A180   D. A325

20. Construction contracts in a broad sense fall into two   20.___
    categories - fixed price and
    A. cost-plus
    B. fixed price plus overhead and profit
    C. negotiated price
    D. arbitrated price

21. A punch list on a construction job is usually made by the   21.___
    inspector
    A. weekly
    B. monthly
    C. continuously during the last half of the job
    D. near the end of the job

22. When an accident occurs on a construction job in which   22.___
    someone is injured, an accident report is usually made
    out by the
    A. insurance carrier   B. contractor
    C. inspector   D. inspector's superior

23. The inspector and the contractor share common goals. The   23.___
    one of the goals listed below that is NOT shared by the
    contractor and the inspector is
    A. get a good job done
    B. see that the contractor makes a reasonable profit
    C. get the job done as speedily as possible
    D. have the job done at as low a cost as possible

24. A crack relief layer is placed over an existing Portland   24.___
    cement concrete pavement followed by a well-graded inter-
    mediate course, then a dense graded surface course.
    The crack relief layer consists of an open graded
        A. mix of 100% crushed material with 25-35% inter-
           connected voids
        B. crushed material heavily compacted with no binder
        C. hot mix made up of 80% crushed material with 20%
           shredded rubber
        D. dense crushed material with voids filled by asphalt

25. Most of the major work performed on the nation's bridges   25.___
    involves
        A. painting the bridges
        B. upgrading the bridges to carry heavier loads
        C. replacing the concrete decks
        D. replacing the suspenders on cable supported bridges

---

KEY (CORRECT ANSWERS)

1. C		11. A	
2. C		12. B	
3. D		13. B	
4. D		14. D	
5. A		15. B	
6. C		16. B	
7. D		17. D	
8. B		18. C	
9. A		19. D	
10. D		20. A	

21. D
22. B
23. B
24. A
25. C

EXAMINATION SECTION
TEST 1

DIRECTIONS: Each question or incomplete statement is followed by several suggested answers or completions. Select the one that BEST answers the question or completes the statement. *PRINT THE LETTER OF THE CORRECT ANSWER IN THE SPACE AT THE RIGHT.*

1. The specifications denote the ultimate strength of concrete at the end of _____ days.   1.___
   A. 7   B. 14   C. 21   D. 28

2. The one of the following that is NOT a purpose of adding an admixture to the concrete mixture is   2.___
   A. set retardation   B. water reduction
   C. required air content   D. increase hardness

3. When a highway slab is to be placed by slipform paving, it is essential that the concrete mix have a   3.___
   A. large slump   B. small slump
   C. high air content   D. low air content

4. Of the following, the accepted method used to insure that the thickness of a sidewalk slab meets the specified minimum depth is to   4.___
   A. have the contractor certify that it meets the specified required depth
   B. measure the depth of the slab at its edge
   C. take a core boring of the slab
   D. place a test load on a square foot of the slab to insure the slab has an adequate bearing capacity

5. Calcium chloride is sometimes added to a concrete mix as a(n) _____ agent.   5.___
   A. retarding   B. air entraining
   C. curing   D. accelerating

6. *Pumping* in a highway concrete slab refers to the   6.___
   A. ejection of water and soil along the edges of a concrete slab
   B. raising of a concrete highway slab due to frost heave
   C. bulging of a concrete slab when high temperature causes excessive expansion of a slab at an expansion joint
   D. raising and falling of a concrete slab caused by a rise in the water table

7. The material used in madjacking consists primarily of _____ sand, cement and water.   7.___
   A. gypsum, coarse   B. coarse
   C. gypsum, fine   D. fine

8. A gallon of water weighs _____ pounds per cubic foot.   8.__
    A. 8.00   B. 8.15   C. 8.33   D. 8.45

9. Of the following, the one that would NOT be used as a   9.__
dust palliative on a road surface would be
    A. calcium sulfate   B. calcium chloride
    C. sodium chloride   D. bituminous substances

10. One of the items in highway maintenance is *soil*   10.__
sterilants. The primary purpose of soil sterilants is to
    A. prevent the spread of mosquitos
    B. prevent the growth of weeds
    C. discourage wild animals from using the road
    D. encourage the growth of wild flowers

Questions 11-16.

DIRECTION: Questions 11 through 16, inclusive, refer to the
following chart describing the gradation of a subbase
for a highway pavement.

Sieve Size Designation	Percent Passing By Weight
75mm	100
50mm	90-100
6.3mm	30-65
425µmm	5-40
75µmm	0-10

11. The maximum percent that can be retained on the 50mm   11.__
screen is
    A. 0   B. 5   C. 10   D. 15

12. The maximum percent that can be retained on the 6.3mm   12.__
screen is
    A. 40   B. 50   C. 60   D. 70

13. The minimum percent that must be retained on the 6.3mm   13.__
screen is
    A. 20   B. 25   C. 30   D. 60

14. The maximum size of aggregate for the subbase is MOST   14.__
NEARLY _____ inches.
    A. 2   B. $2\frac{1}{2}$ C. 3   D. $3\frac{1}{2}$

15. µmm is equal to a _____ of a meter.   15.__
    A. thousandth   B. ten-thousandth
    C. hundred thousandth   D. millionth

16. µ in the metric system is a prefix for   16.__
    A. milli   B. micro   C. nano   D. pico

17. The specifications state that sodium chloride shall be packed in moisture-proof bags not containing more than 45 kg each.
    The MAXIMUM weight per bag, in pounds, is
       A. 95   B. 97   C. 99   D. 101   17._____

18. In placing corrugated steel pipe with longitudinal seams, the longitudinal seams shall be placed   18._____
       A. at the sides of the pipe
       B. at the top of the pipe
       C. at the bottom of the pipe
       D. wherever it is convenient for the contractor

19. In placing corrugated steel pipe, the circumferential seams with laps shall be placed with   19._____
       A. one lap facing upstream and the next lap facing downstream
       B. laps facing in the downstream direction
       C. laps facing in the upstream direction
       D. laps lap welded to the adjacent pipe

20. Before laying corrugated steel pipe, the specifications require that the contractor shall provide the inspector equipment to measure the gauge of the pipe.   20._____
    The equipment referred to is a
       A. micrometer
       B. steel rule that measures to a 64th of an inch
       C. manometer
       D. caliper

21. The thickness of the galvanized coating on a corrugated steel pipe can be measured with a(n)   21._____
       A. fixed probe magnetic gauge
       B. ultrasonic probe
       C. laser gauge
       D. piezometer

22. Terne plate is steel plate coated with   22._____
       A. zinc   B. lead   C. copper   D. tin

23. The cross-section area of a No. 9 reinforcing steel bar is _____ square inches.   23._____
       A. .60   B. .875   C. 1.00   D. 1.128

24. The weight per foot of a No. 9 reinforcing bar is MOST NEARLY _____ pounds per foot.   24._____
       A. 1.8   B. 2.04   C. 3.4   D. 3.64

25. The diameter of a No. 9 bar is _____ inch(es).   25._____
       A. 0.75   B. 0.875   C. 1   D. 1.125

KEY (CORRECT ANSWERS)

1.	D	11.	C
2.	D	12.	D
3.	B	13.	B
4.	C	14.	C
5.	D	15.	D
6.	A	16.	B
7.	D	17.	C
8.	C	18.	A
9.	A	19.	B
10.	B	20.	D

21. A
22. D
23. C
24. C
25. D

TEST 2

DIRECTIONS: Each question or incomplete statement is followed by
several suggested answers or completions. Select the
one that BEST answers the question or completes the
statement. *PRINT THE LETTER OF THE CORRECT ANSWER IN
THE SPACE AT THE RIGHT.*

1. A reinforcing steel bar is designated Grade 40. The 40   1.___
    refers to its
    A. allowable working stress
    B. yield point
    C. elastic limit
    D. ultimate strength

2. The epoxy coating of a reinforcing bar is tested by   2.___
    bending the bar 120° about a mandrel of specified
    diameter. This test is defined as a(n) _____ test.
    A. adhesion   B. tensile   C. shear   D. bearing

3. The hourly rate of flow of sewage is not constant but   3.___
    varies between _____ percent of the daily average.
    A. 90 to 110 B. 70 to 130 C. 50 to 150 D. 30 to 170

4. If the slope of a sewer pipe is .003. The change in   4.___
    elevation in 100 feet is
    A. 3½"   B. 3 5/8"   C. 3 3/4"   D. 4"

5. The minimum allowable velocities in sanitary sewers is   5.___
    _____ feet per second.
    A. 1 to 1.5   B. 1.5 to 2   C. 2.0 to 2.5 D. 2.5 to 3.0

6. Catch basins are designed to   6.___
    A. slow down the flow of storm water
    B. filter out organic material from the storm water
    C. clean grit before it enters the storm sewer
    D. catch grit admitted through street inlets and
       prevent it from entering the storm water drains

7. Before workmen go into a manhole to do repair work, it is   7.___
    necessary to suck out the air from the manhole and replace
    it with fresh air. The MAIN purpose of replacing the
    air in the sewer manhole is to remove
    A. methane gas   B. carbon dioxide
    C. carbon disulfide   D. hydrogen disulfide

8. Sewage consists primarily of fresh water and has less   8.___
    than _____ percent of solid matter.
    A. 0.1   B. 0.2   C. 0.3   D. 0.4

9. Fresh sewage has only a slight odor, but when stale it
    becomes septic and has a strong _____ odor.   9.___
        A. vinegary   B. sweetish
        C. benzene   D. hydrogen sulfide

Questions 10-11.

DIRECTIONS: Questions 10 and 11 refer to the section of an
             existing concrete sewer.

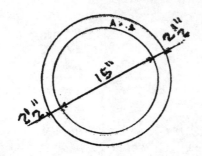

10. If the elevation of the top of the sewer is 24,572 feet,   10.___
    the elevation of the invert of the sewer is _____ feet.
        A. 23.114   B. 23.052   C. 22.965   D. 22.905

11. The cross-section area of the concrete section is sq.in.
        A. 131.5   B. 133.5   C. 135.5   D. 137.5

12. The reason for using wellpoints in the construction of   12.___
    sewers is usually to
        A. prevent the formation of boils
        B. lower the water table
        C. overcome the existence of quicksand
        D. keep the trench dry in the event of a rainstorm

13. Shown at the right is a sewer section   13.___
    with a concrete cradle. The area of
    the cradle is _____ square feet.
        A. 1.60
        B. 1.66
        C. 1.72
        D. 1.78

14.   14.___

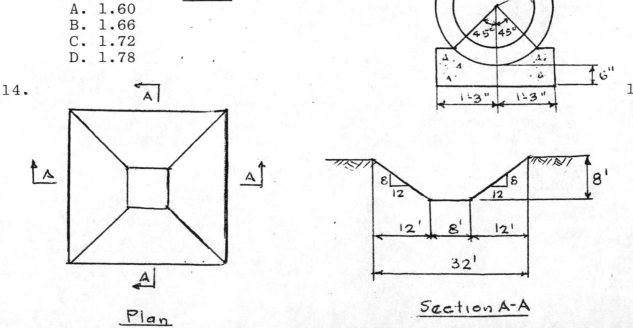

Plan   Section A-A

The volume of excavation by the prismoidal formula is
_____ cubic yards.
   A. 118   B. 123   C. 128   D. 133

15.

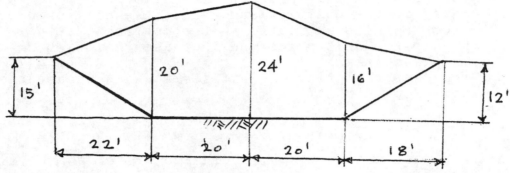

Shown above is the cut for a new highway at a given
station. The area of the cut is _____ square feet.
   A. 1204   B. 1224   C. 1244   D. 1264

16. The number of gallons of water in a cubic foot is
   A. 7.33   B. 7.48   C. 8.00   D. 8.33

Questions 17-18.

DIRECTIONS: Questions 17 and 18 refer to a section across a
           city street.

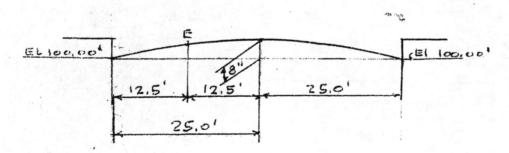

17. If the curve of the road is a parabola, the elevation
of the road at point E is
   A. 100.45   B. 100.50   C. 100.55   D. 100.60

18. The slope of the road at E is _____ percent.
   A. 2.00   B. 2.471   C. 2.667   D. 2.833

19. The universal lane width for a highway is _____ feet.
   A. 10 to 11   B. 11 to 12   C. 12 to 13   D. 13 to 14

15.___

16.___

17.___

18.___

19.___

20. In unit price and lump sum contracts, contractors sometimes
    A. reduce the unit price on items to be carried out early in the project and increase the unit price on items to be carried out later in the contract
    B. increase the unit price on items to be carried out early in the contract and reduce the unit price on items carried out later in the contract
    C. reduce the unit price and increase the price on lump sum items
    D. increase the price on unit items and decrease the price on lump sum items

20.___

Questions 21 to 23.

DIRECTIONS: Questions 21 to 23, inclusive, refer to the diagram below.

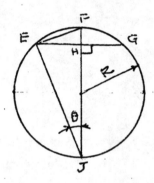

21. EF is equal to
    A. 2R sinθ   B. 2R cosθ   C. 2R tanθ   D. 2R cotθ

21.___

22. EH is equal to
    A. R sin 2θ   B. R cos 2θ   C. R tan 2θ   D. R cot 2θ

22.___

23. FH is equal to

    A. $2R \sin\theta \cos\frac{\theta}{2}$ B. $2R \sin\frac{\theta}{2} \cos\theta$

    C. $2R \sin^2\theta$ D. $2R \cos\theta \cos\frac{\theta}{2}$

23.___

24. The specifications state that the temperature shall be above 10°C. The temperature, in degrees Fahrenheit, is
    A. 40   B. 45   C. 50   D. 55

24.___

25. In a welding electrode designated by four numbers, the strength of the material in the electrode is shown in the _____ number(s).
    A. first   B. first two
    C. first three   D. four

25.___

KEY (CORRECT ANSWERS)

1.	B	11.	D
2.	A	12.	B
3.	C	13.	C
4.	B	14.	D
5.	C	15.	A
6.	D	16.	B
7.	A	17.	B
8.	A	18.	C
9.	D	19.	C
10.	A	20.	B

21. A
22. A
23. C
24. C
25. B

TEST 3

DIRECTIONS: Each question or incomplete statement is followed by several suggested answers or completions. Select the one that BEST answers the question or completes the statement. *PRINT THE LETTER OF THE CORRECT ANSWER IN THE SPACE AT THE RIGHT.*

1. Of the following elements, the one that is harmful in steel is   1.___
   A. molybdenum   B. vandium
   C. silicon   D. phosphorus

2. The size of a fillet weld shown at the right is designated by   2.___
   A. A
   B. B
   C. C
   D. D

   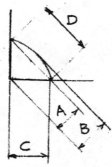

3. The circle on the welding symbol means   3.___
   A. weld in shop
   B. weld in field
   C. plug weld
   D. weld all around

   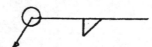

4. Stainless steel is designated as 18-8. The steel contains   4.___
   A. 18% vanadium, 8% chromium
   B. 18% chromium, 8% vanadium
   C. 18% nickel, 8% chromium
   D. 18% chromium, 8% nickel

5. Asphalt cements can be designated by one of two methods. One is viscosity, and the other is   5.___
   A. liquidity   B. penetration
   C. elasticity   D. ductility

6. Paving asphalts are measured by viscosity. A unit measure of absolute viscosity is   6.___
   A. poise   B. tesla   C. oersted   D. pascal

7. The one of the following solvents that is NOT used in   7.____
   cutback asphalt is
       A. naphtha   B. gasoline   C. toluene   D. kerosene

8. The advantage of using cutback asphalt over ordinary   8.____
   asphalt is that cutback asphalt _____ than ordinary
   asphalt.
       A. has a higher viscosity
       B. cures more slowly
       C. can be applied at a temperature lower
       D. produces a harder surface

9. When excavating for a roadway, the volume of excavation   9.____
   removed becomes greater than the volume of the earth
   before removal. The percent of increase in volume is
   termed
       A. swell   B. expansion
       C. blow-up   D. displacement

10. The approximate increase in volume when dry sand is   10.____
    excavated is MOST NEARLY _____ percent.
        A. 2   B. 20   C. 28   D. 36

11. The tolerance for the elevation of the base of a pavement   11.____
    is ± .02 feet. In the metric system, this would be
        A. ±4   B. ±6   C. ±8   D. ±10

12. When the areas of a road surface to be patched are   12.____
    numerous, or they extend over a considerable area, it
    is often more efficient to recondition the entire
    surface.
    The usual procedure is to _____ the surface of the road-
    way to the full depth of the surface material.
        A. excavate   B. eviscerate
        C. scarify   D. plow

13. The ASTM defines a permeable textile material or any   13.____
    other geotechnical engineering-related material as a
        A. geomorphic material
        B. synthetic permeable textile
        C. geomorphic reinforcement
        D. geotextile

14. In wood terminology, a shake is a   14.____
        A. variation from a true or plane surface
        B. separation along the grain
        C. deviation edgewise from a straight line drawn from
           end to end of a piece
        D. lack of wood or bark from any cause

15. The primary difference between heartwood and sapwood is   15.____
    that
        A. heartwood is stronger than sapwood
        B. sapwood is stronger than heartwood
        C. sapwood is more susceptible to decay than heartwood
        D. sapwood is normally darker than heartwood

16. The specific gravity of southern yellow pine based on   16.___
    oven-dry weight and volume is
       A. .38   B. .48   C. .58   D. .68

17. The length of a 10 penny nail is _____ inches.   17.___
       A. 3   B. $3\frac{1}{4}$ C. $3\frac{1}{2}$ D. 4

18. The specifications state that in extreme situations   18.___
    face brick may be cleaned with a 5% solution of muriatic
    acid. Muriatic acid is another name for _____ acid.
       A. sulfuric   B. hydrochloric
       C. acetic   D. hydrofluoric

19. The main advantage of CPM over the traditional bar chart   19.___
    in scheduling a construction project is that CPM can
    more easily
       A. procure material
       B. eliminate potential bottlenecks during construction
       C. improve safety on the project
       D. eliminate unnecessary work to complete the project

20. In CPM, the float is   20.___
       A. positive in the critical path
       B. negative in the critical path
       C. 0 in the critical path
       D. positive or negative in the critical path, depending
          on whether the project is ahead of schedule or
          behind schedule

21. In CPM, the float in a given activity is the   21.___
       A. uncertainty when the activity can be finished without
          delaying the project
       B. uncertainty as to how much time is needed to complete
          the activity
       C. period during which the activity can be started with-
          out delaying the project
       D. flexibility needed to complete the activity without
          delaying the project

22. The GREATEST source of construction-related claims for   22.___
    additional payment for contractors and cost overruns
    result from
       A. labor strikes
       B. errors in design
       C. unanticipated soil conditions
       D. faulty material

23. High early strength cement is used in a concrete mix   23.___
    whenever the extra cost is offset by the value of the
    earlier use of the structure. The use of additional
    Portland cement in a mix gives high early strength, but
    has the disadvantage of

A. causing segregation when placing the concrete
B. having reduced strength over a longer period of time
C. requires more fine aggregates
D. causing greater shrinkage of the mass in curing

24. Special cements are designed specifically to resist   24.___
    chemical attack. The chemical group it is designed to
    resist are
    A. chlorates   B. sulfates
    C. nitrates   D. carbonates

25. Of the following, the synthetic fiber LEAST likely to   25.___
    raise loads in slings is
    A. nylon   B. orlon
    C. polyester   D. polypropylene

KEY (CORRECT ANSWERS)

1. D		11. B	
2. C		12. C	
3. D		13. D	
4. D		14. B	
5. B		15. C	
6. A		16. C	
7. C		17. A	
8. C		18. B	
9. A		19. B	
10. A		20. C	

21. C
22. C
23. D
24. B
25. B

TEST 4

DIRECTIONS: Each question or incomplete statement is followed by several suggested answers or completions. Select the one that BEST answers the question or completes the statement. *PRINT THE LETTER OF THE CORRECT ANSWER IN THE SPACE AT THE RIGHT.*

1. Of the following liquids, the one that has the LOWEST viscosity is
   A. alcohol
   B. water
   C. raw petroleum
   D. glycerin

   1.___

2. The inspector uses a sling psychrometer in check painting to check the
   A. density of the paint
   B. viscosity of the paint
   C. moisture in the air
   D. barometric pressure

   2.___

3. Of the following tests on structural steel, the one that is NOT non-destructive is
   A. radiographic
   B. ultrasonic
   C. magnetic particle
   D. tensile

   3.___

4. Which of the following is a high strength bolt?
   A. A7   B. A36   C. A325   D. A502

   4.___

5. The size of hole for a 3/4 inch bolt is

   A. $\frac{3"}{4}$ B. $\frac{13"}{32}$ C. $\frac{13"}{16}$ D. $\frac{27"}{32}$

   5.___

6. Foam fire extinguishers are unsuitable to fight _____ fires.
   A. wood
   B. paper
   C. flammable liquid
   D. electric equipment

   6.___

7. Of the following types of fire extinguishers, the one MOST suitable to fight wood and paper fires is
   A. water type-soda acid
   B. carbon dioxide
   C. sodium bicarbonate-dry chemical
   D. potassium bicarbonate-dry chemical

   7.___

8. A multi-purpose fire extinguisher is
   A. foam
   B. carbon dioxide
   C. ABC
   D. soda acid

   8.___

9. The fire extinguisher with the SHORTEST range is 9.___
   A. cartridge operated   B. soda acid
   C. carbon dioxide   D. stored pressure

10. The Occupational Safety and Health Act Part 1926 states 10.___
that all trenches and earth embankments over _____ feet
deep be adequately protected against caving in.
   A. 4   B. 5   C. 6   D. 7

11. During excavation, most cave-ins occur 11.___
   A. when excavating for retaining walls
   B. during cold weather
   C. in shallow excavations
   D. in the western part of the United States

12. _____ soils are MOST susceptible to cave-ins. 12.___
   A. All   B. Clayey   C. Silty   D. Sandy

13. In highway construction work, material required for 13.___
earthwork construction in excess of the quantity of
suitable material available from the required grading,
cuts and elevations is known as
   A. overhaul   B. deficit
   C. borrow   D. shrinkage

14. The number of strands in manila rope is USUALLY 14.___
   A. 2   B. 3   C. 4   D. 5

15. The factor of safety for manila rope is 15.___
   A. 3   B. 5   C. 7   D. 9

Questions 16-20.

DIRECTIONS: Questions 16 through 20, inclusive, refer to a
section through a 20'-0" long reinforced concrete
retaining wall.

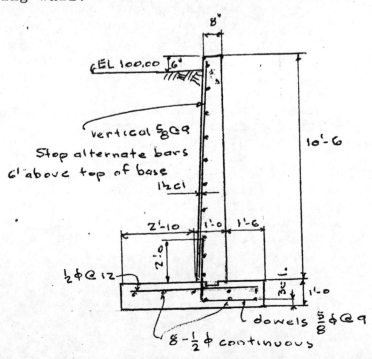

16. The slope of the inclined wall is MOST NEARLY
    A. 1/8 inch on 12"   B. 1/4 inch on 12"
    C. 3/8 inch on 12"   D. 1/2 inch on 12"
    16.___

17. The volume of concrete in the vertical wall is _____
cubic yards.
    A. 5.9   B. 6.1   C. 6.3   D. 6.5
    17.___

18. The elevation of the bottom of the footing is
    A. 89.00'   B. 89.500'   C. 90.00'   D. 90.5'
    18.___

19. The number of dowels $\frac{5}{8}\phi$ @ a is

    A. 23   B. 25   C. 27   D. 29
    19.___

20. The number of vertical $\frac{5}{8}\phi$ @a that are the full height
of the wall is
    A. 12   B. 14   C. 16   D. 27
    20.___

21. A state highway contract contains a Buy America clause.
The material referred to in the clause is MOST NEARLY
    A. cement   B. lumber
    C. aluminum   D. steel
    21.___

22. In a unit price contract where additional work does not
fall under any item, the extra work is to be paid on a
cost-plus basis. If the contractor uses his own crane,
he is entitled to the
    A. cost of operating the crane only
    B. cost of operating the crane and servicing the crane
       only
    C. rental cost of the crane, the cost of operating the
       crane, and the cost of servicing the crane only
    D. cost of repairing the crane if the crane is damaged
       and the cost of operating and servicing the crane
       only
    22.___

23. The delivery ticket for a truck delivering bituminous
pavement mixture contains an entry "Tare Weight." Tare
weight on the ticket refers to the
    A. correction for the scales weighing the bituminous
       mixture
    B. truck weight without load
    C. weight of fuel on the truck
    D. truck weight with load
    23.___

24. The PRIMARY difference between silt and loam is that
    A. silt contains some organic material
    B. loam contains some organic material
    C. silt consists primarily of clay
    D. loam consists primarily of clay
    24.___

25. A recent development in high strength concrete is _____   25.___
     concrete.
         A. silica fume   B. low slump
         C. fly ash   D. finely ground cement

KEY (CORRECT ANSWERS)

1. A		11. C	
2. C		12. A	
3. D		13. C	
4. C		14. B	
5. B		15. B	
6. D		16. C	
7. A		17. D	
8. C		18. A	
9. C		19. C	
10. B		20. B	

21. D
22. C
23. B
24. B
25. A

EXAMINATION SECTION
TEST 1

DIRECTIONS: Each question or incomplete statement is followed by several suggested answers or completions. Select the one that BEST answers the question or completes the statement. *PRINT THE LETTER OF THE CORRECT ANSWER IN THE SPACE AT THE RIGHT.*

1. Management by exception (MBE) is

    A. designed to locate bottlenecks
    B. designed to pinpoint superior performance
    C. a form of index locating
    D. a form of variance reporting

1.____

2. In managerial terms, gap analysis is useful primarily in

    A. problem solving   B. setting standards
    C. inventory control   D. locating bottlenecks

2.____

3. ABC analysis involves

    A. problem solving   B. indexing
    C. brainstorming   D. inventory control

3.____

4. The Federal Discrimination in Employment Act as amended in 1978 prohibits job discrimination based on age for persons between the ages of

    A. 35 and 60   B. 40 and 65   C. 45 and 65   D. 40 and 70

4.____

5. Inspectors should be familiar with the contractor's CPM charts for a construction job primarily to determine if

    A. the job is on schedule
    B. the contractor is using the charts correctly
    C. material is on hand to keep the job on schedule
    D. there is a potential source of delay

5.____

6. The value engineering approach is frequently found in public works contracts. Value engineering is

    A. an effort to cut down or eliminate extra work payments
    B. a team approach to optimize the cost of the project
    C. to insure that material and equipment will perform as specified
    D. to insure that insurance costs on the project can be minimized

6.____

7. Historically, most costly claims have been either for

    A. unreasonable inspection requirements or unforeseen weather conditions
    B. unreasonable specification requirements or unreasonable completion time for the contract
    C. added costs due to inflation or unavailability of material
    D. delays or alleged changed conditions

7.____

8.   A claim is a

8.__

    A.   dispute that cannot be resolved
    B.   dispute arising from ambiguity in the specifications
    C.   dispute arising from the quality of the work
    D.   recognition that the courts are the sole arbiters of a dispute

9.   Disputes arising between a contractor and the owning agency are

9.__

    A.   the result of inflexibility of either or both parties to the dispute
    B.   mainly the result of shortcomings in the design
    C.   the result of shortcomings in the specifications
    D.   inevitable

Questions 10-13.

DIRECTIONS: Questions 10 through 13, inclusive, refers to the array of numbers listed below.

    16, 7, 9, 5, 10, 8, 5, 1, 2

10.   The mean of the numbers is

10.__

    A. 2   B. 5   C. 7   D. 8

11.   The median of the numbers is

11.__

    A. 2   B. 5   C. 7   D. 8

12.   The mode of the numbers is

12.__

    A. 2   B. 5   C. 7   D. 8

13.   In statistical measurements, a subgroup that is representative of the entire group is a

13.__

    A.   commutative group   B.   sample
    C.   central index   D.   Abelian group

14.   Productivity is the ratio of

14.__

    A. $\dfrac{\text{product costs}}{\text{labor costs}}$

    B. $\dfrac{\text{cost of final product}}{\text{cost of materials}}$

    C. $\dfrac{\text{outputs}}{\text{inputs}}$

    D. $\dfrac{\text{outputs cost}}{\text{time needed to product the output}}$

15.   Downtime is the time a piece of equipment is

15.__

    A.   idle waiting for other equipment to become available
    B.   not being used for the purpose it was intended

C. being used inefficiently
D. unavailable for use

16. Index numbers   16._____

    A. relates to the cost of a product as material costs vary
    B. allows the user to find the variation from the norm
    C. are a way of comparing costs of different approaches to a problem
    D. a way of measuring and comparing changes over a period of time

17. The underlying idea behind Management by Objectives is to provide a mechanism for   17._____
managers to

    A. coordinate personal and departmental plans with organizational goals
    B. motivate employees by having them participate in job decisions
    C. motivate employees by training them for the next higher position
    D. set objectives that are reasonable for the employees to attain, thus improving self-esteem among the employees

18. The ultimate objective of the project manager in planning and scheduling a project is to   18._____

    A. meet the completion dates of the project
    B. use the least amount of labor on the project
    C. use the least amount of material on the project
    D. prevent interference between the different trades

19. Scheduling with respect to the critical path method usually does not involve   19._____

    A. cost allocation
    B. starting and finishing time
    C. float for each activity
    D. project duration

20. When CPM is used on a construction project, updates are most commonly made   20._____

    A. weekly   B. every two weeks
    C. monthly   D. every two months

Questions 21-24.

DIRECTIONS: Questions 21 through 24 refer to the following network.

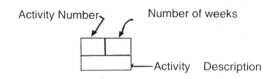

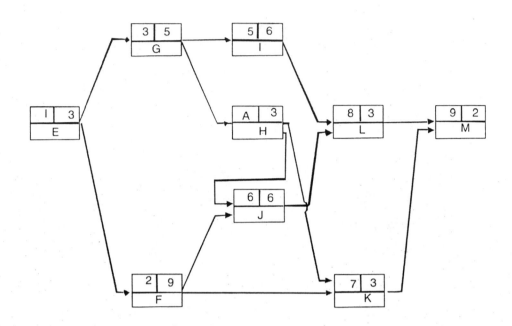

Activity Number	Activity Description	Duration in Weeks	Early Start	Early Finish	Late Start	Late Finish	Total Slack
1	E	3					
2	F	9					
3	G	5					
4	H	3					
5	I	6					
6	J	6					
7	K	3					
8	L	3					
9	M	2					

21. The critical path is   21.___

    A. E G H J L M   B. E G I L M
    C. E F J L M   D. E G H K M

22. The minimum time needed to complete the job is, in weeks,   22.___

    A. 19   B. 21   C. 22   D. 23

23. The slack time in J is, in weeks,   23.___

    A. 0   B. 1   C. 2   D. 3

24. The slack time in K is, in weeks,   24.___

    A. 4   B. 5   C. 6   D. 7

25. Of the following, the primary objective of CPM is to   25.____

    A. eliminate duplication of work
    B. overcome obstacles such as bad weather
    C. spot potential bottlenecks
    D. save on the cost of material

_____

KEY (CORRECT ANSWERS)

1.	D		11.	C
2.	A		12.	B
3.	D		13.	B
4.	D		14.	C
5.	A		15.	D
6.	B		16.	D
7.	D		17.	A
8.	A		18.	A
9.	D		19.	A
10.	C		20.	C

21.	C
22.	D
23.	A
24.	C
25.	C

_____

TEST 2

DIRECTIONS: Each question or incomplete statement is followed by several suggested answers or completions. Select the one that BEST answers the question or completes the statement. *PRINT THE LETTER OF THE CORRECT ANSWER IN THE SPACE AT THE RIGHT.*

1. Gantt refers to

    A. bar charts
    C. PERT networks
    B. milestone charts
    D. Management by Objectives

1.___

2. PERT is an abbreviation for

    A. Progress Evaluation in Real Time
    B. Preliminary Evaluation of Running Time
    C. Program Evaluation Review Techniques
    D. Program Estimation and Repair Times

2.___

3. In project management terms, slack is equivalent to

    A. tare   B. off time   C. delay   D. float

3.___

4. The FIRST step in planning and programming a roadway pavement management system is to evaluate

    A. priorities for the work to be done
    B. the condition of your equipment
    C. the condition of the roads in the system
    D. the storage and maintenance facilities

4.___

5. Managers accomplish their work in an ever changing environment by integrating three time-tested approaches. The one of the following that is NOT a time-tested approach is

    A. scientific adaptation
    C. behavior management
    B. scientific management
    D. management sciences

5.___

6. The most effective managers manage for optimum results. This means that the manager is seeking to _____ a given situation.

    A. get the maximum results from
    B. get the most favorable results from
    C. get the most reasonable results from
    D. satisfy the conflicting interests in

6.___

7. If a manager believes that an employee is irresponsible, the employee, in subtle response to the manager's assessment, will in fact prove to be irresponsible. This is an example of a(n)

    A. conditioned reflex
    C. Freudian response
    B. self-fulfilling prophesy
    D. automatic reaction

7.___

8. Perhaps nothing distinguishes the younger generation from the older so much as the value placed on work. The older generation was generally raised to believe in the Protestant work ethic.
This ethic holds primarily that

8.___

A. people should try to get the highest salary possible
B. work should help people to advance
C. work should be well done if it is interesting
D. work is valuable in itself and the person who does it focuses on his work

9. The standard method currently in use in inspecting bituminous paving is to inspect each activity in detail as the paving work is being installed. In recent years some agencies use a different method of inspection known as a(n)   9._____

A. as-built quality control method
B. statistically controlled quality assurance method
C. data based history of previous contracts of this type
D. performance evaluation of the completed paving contract

10. Aggregates for use in bituminous pavements should be tested for grading,   10._____

A. abrasion, soundness, and specific gravity
B. type of rock, abrasion, and specific gravity
C. abrasion, soundness, and deleterious material
D. specific gravity, chemical composition of the aggregate, and deleterious material

11. Of the following, the one that is LEAST likely to be a test for asphalt is   11._____

A. specific gravity   B. flashpoint
C. viscosity   D. penetration

12. According to the AASHO, for bituminous pavements PSI is an abbreviation for _____ Index.   12._____

A. Present Serviceability   B. Pavement Smoothness
C. Pavement Serviceability   D. Present Smoothness

13. According to the AASHO, a bituminous pavement that is in extremely poor condition will have a PSI   13._____

A. above 5.5   B. above 3.5
C. below 3.5   D. below 1.5

14. The U.S. Federal Highway Administration defines asphalt maintenance as including work designed primarily for rejuvenation or protection of existing surfaces less than _____ inch minimum thickness.   14._____

A. 1/4   B. 1/2   C. 3/4   D. 1

15. The maintenance phase of a highway management system includes the establishment of a program and schedule of work based largely on budget considerations, the actual operations of crack filling, patching, etc. and   15._____

A. inspection of completed work
B. planning of future operations
C. upgrading existing pavements
D. acquisition and processing of data

16. In a bituminous asphalt pavement, the progressive separation of aggregate particles in a pavement from the surface downward or from the edges inward is the definition of

    A. alligatoring   B. raveling
    C. scaling   D. disintegration

16.___

17. The bituminous pavement condition for the purpose of overlay design includes ride quality, structural capacity, skid resistance, and

    A. durability   B. age of the pavement
    C. CBR value   D. surface distress

17.___

18. An asphalt mix is being transferred from an asphalt truck to the hopper of the paving machine. Blue smoke rises from the material being emptied into the hopper of the paving machine.
Your conclusion should be that

    A. this is normal and is to be expected
    B. the mix is overheated
    C. the mix is too cold
    D. the mix is being transferred too rapidly

18.___

19. Polished aggregate in an asphalt pavement are aggregate particles that have been rounded and polished smooth by traffic. This is a

    A. *good* condition as it allows a smooth ride
    B. *good* condition as it preserves tires
    C. *poor* condition as it promotes skidding
    D. *poor* condition as it tends to break the bond between the asphalt and the aggregate

19.___

20. A slippery asphalt surface requires a skid-resistant surfacing material. Of the following, the cover that would be most appropriate is a(n)

    A. asphalt tack coat
    B. fog seal
    C. layer of sand rolled into the asphalt surface
    D. asphalt emulsion slurry seal

20.___

21. The maximum size of aggregate in a hot mix asphalt concrete surfacing and bases allowed by the Federal Highway Administration Grading A is _____ inch(es).

    A. 3/4   B. 1   C. 1 1/4   D. 1 1/2

21.___

22. Wet sand weighs 132 pounds per cubic foot and contains 8% noisture. The dry weight of a cubic foot of sand is _____ pounds.

    A. 122.2   B. 122.0   C. 121.7   D. 121.4

22.___

23. A very light spray application of 551h emulsified asphalt diluted with water is used on existing pavement as a seal to riinimize raveling and to enrich the surface of a dried-out pavement is known as a(n)

    A. prime coat   B. tack coat
    C. fog seal   D. emulsion seal

23.___

24. 90 kilometers per hour is equivalent to _____ miles per hour.   24._____

    A. 49   B. 54   C. 59   D. 64

25. In a table of pavement distress manifestations is a column broadly titled *Density of Pave-*   25._____
    ment Distress.
    This is equivalent to _____ of the defects.

    A. average depth   B. average area
    C. extent of occurrence   D. seriousness

———

KEY (CORRECT ANSWERS)

1.	A		11.	A
2.	A		12.	A
3.	D		13.	D
4.	C		14.	C
5.	A		15.	D
6.	B		16.	B
7.	B		17.	D
8.	D		18.	B
9.	B		19.	C
10.	C		20.	D

21.	D
22.	A
23.	C
24.	B
25.	C

———

EXAMINATION SECTION
TEST 1

DIRECTIONS: Each question or incomplete statement is followed by several suggested answers or completions. Select the one that BEST answers the question or completes the statement. *PRINT THE LETTER OF THE CORRECT ANSWER IN THE SPACE AT THE RIGHT.*

1. Under conditions of rain and fog, headlights MUST be turned on if visibility is *less than*
   A. 100 feet   B. 500 feet
   C. 1,000 feet   D. 1/4 of a mile

   1.___

2. If a blowout occurs while a vehicle is moving, the driver SHOULD
   A. hold tightly onto the steering wheel and immediately apply steady foot pressure to the brake pedal
   B. hold tightly onto the steering wheel and turn off the roadway as soon as the blowout occurs, stopping the vehicle on the shoulder area
   C. start tapping the brake pedal with his foot, sound his horn to warn others, and move into the slow-moving lane immediately
   D. hold tightly onto the steering wheel, steer straight ahead, and ease up on the accelerator

   2.___

3. Which of the following is NOT a correct action to take after parking on a shoulder of a highway?
   A. Turn on the emergency lights
   B. Have all occupants stay inside the vehicle
   C. Open the hood of the car
   D. Fasten a white cloth to the door handle or radio antenna

   3.___

4. It is officially recommended that drivers stay behind cars in front of them a distance of at least one car length for every ten miles per hour of speed.
   The PRINCIPAL reason for this is to
   A. increase roadway capacity
   B. make it easier for cars to change lanes
   C. allow for enough distance to stop safely if the car ahead stops suddenly
   D. keep all the cars moving at the same speed

   4.___

5. To *minimize* the glare from lights of oncoming cars at night, a driver should
   A. shift his eyes to the lower right side of his traffic lane
   B. blink his eyes frequently
   C. shift his eyes to the upper right side of his traffic lane
   D. use his upper beams to offset the glare

   5.___

6. The number of yards in a mile is   6.___
   A. 5,280   B. 1,760   C. 880   D. 440

7. Vehicle classification data is MOST important in   7.___
   calculating the
   A. capacity of a roadway
   B. timing of traffic signals
   C. turnover of parking in a lot
   D. average speed of travel

8. Condition diagrams show   8.___
   A. the same information as collision diagrams plus
     information about vehicle classification
   B. the same information as collision diagrams plus
     information about vehicle speeds and traffic volumes
   C. traffic volumes only
   D. existing physical features at a location

9. Thirty miles per hour is *equivalent* to _____ feet per   9.___
   second.
   A. 30   B. 44   C. 60   D. 80

10. Origin and destination studies are used CHIEFLY to   10.___
   A. obtain information on travel habits
   B. collect traffic volume data
   C. estimate travel time between cities
   D. determine roadway capacities

11. The BEST way to determine the number of cars parked in   11.___
   an off-street parking lot during a 12-hour period is to
   conduct a(n) _____ study.
   A. parking occupancy   B. vehicle classification
   C. origin/destination   D. parking turnover

12. The BEST way to determine the number of vehicles that   12.___
   have been parked for more than 1 hour within a 1-hour
   parking meter area is to record the _____ every hour.
   A. color of each vehicle parked
   B. license numbers of every parked vehicle
   C. make and year of each car parked
   D. number of violations shown on the meters

13. A traffic flow map is used to show   13.___
   A. speeds along a highway in both directions and at
     intersections
   B. the available capacity on a highway during peak hours
   C. the traffic volumes that pass through an intersection
     or travel along a highway
   D. the one- and two-way street patterns in an area

14. The *running speed* on a highway is the   14.___
   A. posted speed limit
   B. length of the highway divided by the time it takes
     to travel the highway

C. speed for which the highway was designed
D. speed at a specific point along the highway as
determined through a radar speed study

15. The 85 percentile speed on a given stretch of highway for   15.___
a certain period of time is
A. the speed below which 85% of all traffic travels
B. the speed above which 85% of all traffic travels
C. 85% of the posted speed limit
D. 85% of the running speed

16. The *modal* speed on a highway is   16.___
A. average speed traveled by vehicles using the highway
B. speed value which is halfway between the highest and
lowest speed recorded in a speed study
C. average spot speed at a given station on the highway
D. speed value occurring most frequently as recorded in
a speed study

17. For a given number of lanes in a roadway, the capacity   17.___
of the roadway
A. decreases as lane widths decrease
B. increases as lane widths decrease
C. is not affected by lane widths
D. is affected by lane widths only on steep grades

18. Speed and delay studies are used to   18.___
A. determine the number of vehicles traveling above
and below the speed limit
B. establish speed limits
C. identify locations where curb parking needs to be
restricted
D. measure the effectiveness of changes in traffic
signal timing

19. The average annual daily traffic on a highway is the   19.___
A. total yearly volume divided by the number of days
in the year
B. average weekday volume times 365
C. average of the highest and lowest 24-hour volumes
recorded during the year
D. average 24-hour volume recorded exclusive of
Saturdays, Sundays, and holidays

20. Turning movement counts at intersections are USUALLY   20.___
made
A. with the use of mechanical counters
B. with the use of radar detectors
C. by manual means
D. by estimation based upon traffic flow diagrams

21. Under ideal roadway and traffic conditions, the basic capacity for uninterrupted traffic flow conditions for each lane of a multi-lane roadway is _____ passenger cars per hour.
    A. 500 B. 1,000 C. 2,000 D. 4,000

21.___

22. For heavy volumes of mixed traffic, the IDEAL lane width is _____ feet.
    A. 10 B. 12 C. 14 D. 16

22.___

23. When describing highway capacity under various traffic conditions, flow, volumes, and speeds, levels of service definitions are used.
    The level of service which describes a condition on the roadway of free flow, low volume, and high speed is known as level of service
    A. A B. B C. C D. D

23.___

24. The MOST efficient use of space in a rectangular or square-shaped parking lot can USUALLY be arrived at through the use of _____ parking stalls.
    A. parallel
    B. 45-degree
    C. 90-degree
    D. a combination of angle and 90-degree

24.___

25. If a single mechanical traffic counter is installed on each approach to an intersection, the data collected will NOT include
    A. peak hour volumes
    B. the total volumes through the intersection
    C. turning movements
    D. motorcycle traffic

25.___

KEY (CORRECT ANSWERS)

1. C		11. D	
2. D		12. B	
3. B		13. C	
4. C		14. B	
5. A		15. A	
6. B		16. D	
7. A		17. A	
8. D		18. D	
9. B		19. A	
10. A		20. C	

21. C
22. B
23. A
24. C
25. C

TEST 2

DIRECTIONS: Each question or incomplete statement is followed by
several suggested answers or completions. Select the
one that BEST answers the question or completes the
statement. *PRINT THE LETTER OF THE CORRECT ANSWER IN
THE SPACE AT THE RIGHT.*

Questions 1-5.

DIRECTIONS: Questions 1 through 5, inclusive, refer to Figures 1
and 2, which appear below and on the following page.

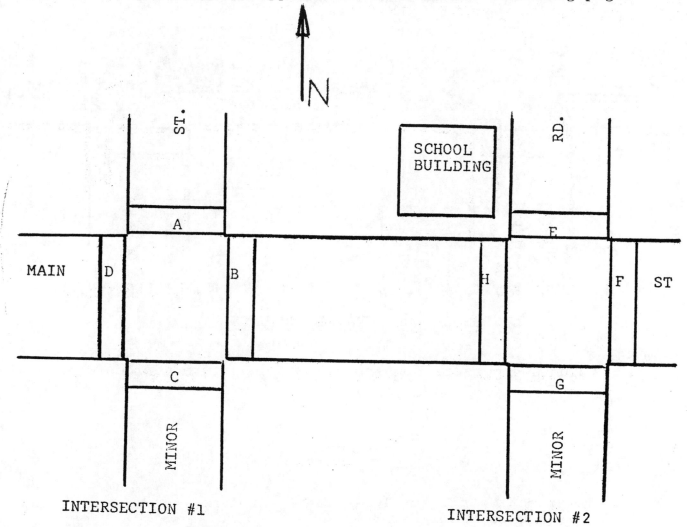

POSSIBLE CROSSWALK LOCATIONS

NOTES	STREET DIRECTIONS
1	Main Street is one-way eastbound
2	Cross Street is two-way
3	Cross Road is one-way northbound
4	Both intersections are uncontrolled

FIGURE 1

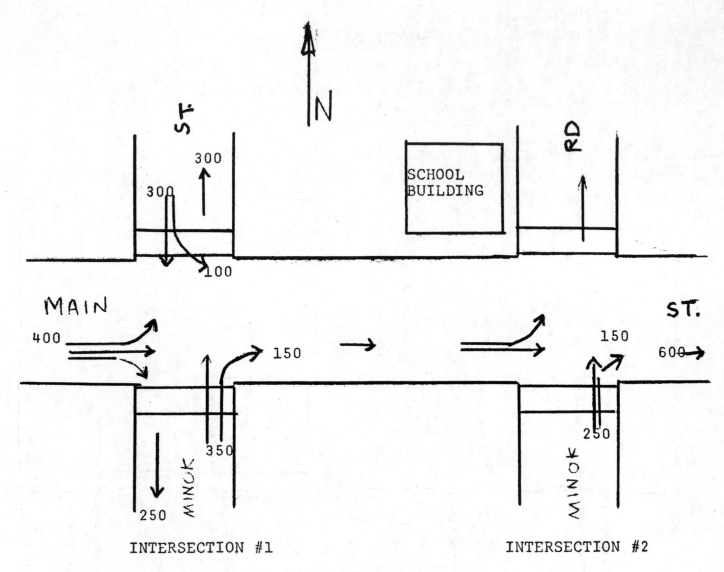

INTERSECTION #1   INTERSECTION #2

SCHOOL HOUR TRAFFIC VOLUMES

NOTE:
   1 Volumes shown are for arrival and departure periods.

FIGURE 2

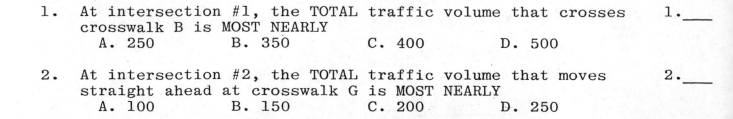

1. At intersection #1, the TOTAL traffic volume that crosses   1.___
    crosswalk B is MOST NEARLY
       A. 250   B. 350   C. 400   D. 500

2. At intersection #2, the TOTAL traffic volume that moves   2.___
    straight ahead at crosswalk G is MOST NEARLY
       A. 100   B. 150   C. 200   D. 250

3. At intersection #1, the TOTAL traffic volume that moves   3.___
   straight ahead at crosswalk D is MOST NEARLY
      A. 150   B. 200   C. 250   D. 300

4. At intersection #2, the crosswalks that should be desig-   4.___
   nated as school crossings are
      A. E, F, G, H   B. E, F, G
      C. E, F, H   D. E, H, G

5. Assuming that only one police officer or school crossing   5.___
   guard can be assigned for school crossing patrol duty,
   the officer or guard should be assigned to intersection
      A. #1 during student arrival periods and at intersec-
         tion #2 during student departure periods
      B. #2 during student arrival periods and at intersec-
         tion #1 during student departure periods
      C. #1 during both arrival and departure periods
      D. #2 during both arrival and departure periods

6. In the city, the CLOSEST a car may be parked to a hydrant   6.___
   is _____ feet.
      A. 5   B. 10   C. 15   D. 20

7. Of the following violations, the one which would NOT be   7.___
   recorded as a penalty on a driver's license is
      A. failure to stop at a stop sign
      B. double parking
      C. front or rear lights not working
      D. passing a red light

8. The current trend in the manufacture of new automobiles   8.___
   in the United States is to
      A. give the new automobiles capacity for higher speeds
      B. make them smaller
      C. restore the running board
      D. give them disappearing front lights

9. Of the following, the statement relating to parking meter   9.___
   spaces adjacent to fire hydrants that is MOST NEARLY
   correct is they
      A. may be made shorter than others in the block
      B. must be at least 25 feet long
      C. cannot be closer than 20 feet to the hydrant
      D. may be within 10 feet of the hydrant

10. In the city, parking signs that prohibit parking are   10.___
    made with _____ letters on a _____ background.
       A. green; white   B. white; green
       C. black; white   D. red; white

11. A driver whose car is parked for 8 hours in an off-street 11.___
    facility where the rate is 50 cents an hour for the first
    5 hours and 75 cents an hour thereafter would pay
       A. $6.00   B. $5.75   C. $4.75   D. $4.00

12. To encourage shoppers and other short-term parkers and
    to discourage commuters from using parking garages in
    the city, it would be BEST to
       A. charge a uniform high hourly rate all day
       B. charge a high rate for the first three to five hours
          and decrease the rate thereafter
       C. charge a lower rate for the first three hours and
          increase the rate sharply thereafter
       D. limit all parking to one-half hour   12.___

13. If an investigation of insufficient parking for customers
    at a busy post office revealed that the only six available
    spaces were occupied by all-day parkers, the recommended
    action should be to
       A. install two-hour parking signs
       B. make the area a No Parking zone
       C. do nothing because the spaces are being used
       D. install 20-minute meters   13.___

14. A street which can accommodate 40 parked trucks along
    both curbs is experiencing congestion problems because
    there are not enough lanes for through traffic. A survey
    reveals stores and businesses along both sides of the
    street and truck parking along both curbs. The total
    number of vehicles parked is never more than 20.
    The recommended action should be to
       A. prohibit truck parking at all times along one curb
       B. prohibit truck parking for the first half of the
          day along one curb and the second half of the day
          along the other curb
       C. prohibit parking on alternate days along each curb
       D. establish loading zones mid-block along each curb   14.___

15. An off-street parking garage where the driver parks his
    own vehicle is called a _____ garage.
       A. self-parking   B. ramp
       C. commuter   D. mechanical   15.___

16. Off-street garages and lots where attendants park vehicles
    need adequate reservoir (storage) space at the entrance
    PRIMARILY to
       A. reduce customer waiting time when picking up cars
       B. reduce the number of attendants needed to park cars
       C. avoid spill-back of cars into the street system
       D. have extra space for parking cars when the garage
          fills up   16.___

17. Parking turnover is defined as the
       A. capacity of a parking lot or garage divided by the
          number of cars parked in it
       B. average number of times a parking space in a parking
          lot or garage is used during a given period of time
       C. number of empty spaces in a parking lot or garage
       D. number of space hours used during a day in a park-
          ing lot or garage   17.___

18. One-half hour parking meters would BEST serve customers   18.___
    of a(n)
    A. supermarket   B. medical building
    C. bank   D. office building

19. An off-street parking facility at a shopping center is   19.___
    operating at its BEST efficiency when it is _____ full.
    A. 100%   B. 85%   C. 75%   D. 50%

20.   20.___

Two types of barriers are shown above, Type X and Type Y.
An *advantage* of Type X barrier over Type Y barrier is
that Type X barrier _____ than Type Y.
    A. has a lower initial cost
    B. is easier to install
    C. requires less maintenance
    D. is more visible

21. A fatality is MOST likely to occur in a _____ accident.   21.___
    A. rear-end   B. right-angle
    C. side-swipe   D. head-on

22. Most accidents USUALLY occur   22.___
    A. during the morning rush hours
    B. at midday
    C. in the late afternoon and early evening
    D. between midnight and dawn

23. For the United States as a whole, studies have shown   23.___
    that alcohol was a contributing factor in _____ of the
    fatal accidents.
    A. 5%   B. 15%   C. 25%   D. 50%

24. The MAIN advantage of a red, yellow, and green light   24.___
    over a red and green light is that the red, yellow, and
    green light
    A. is less expensive
    B. is easier to install
    C. gives the driver warning of a change in signals from
       green to red
    D. gives the police officer firm evidence if he wants
       to issue a violation for passing a light

25. Dividing the total number of accidents occurring in one   25.___
    year on a roadway by the length of the roadway in miles
    will yield the
    A. fatality rate for the roadway
    B. accident rate per annual vehicle miles traveled
    C. accident exposure rate for the roadway
    D. accident rate per mile per year

———

KEY (CORRECT ANSWERS)

1. D		11. C
2. A		12. C
3. C		13. D
4. D		14. B
5. C		15. A
6. C		16. C
7. B		17. B
8. B		18. C
9. A		19. B
10. D		20. C

21. D
22. C
23. D
24. C
25. D

———

EXAMINATION SECTION

TEST 1

DIRECTIONS: Each question or incomplete statement is followed by several suggested answers or completions. Select the one that BEST answers the question or completes the statement. *PRINT THE LETTER OF THE CORRECT ANSWER IN THE SPACE AT THE RIGHT.*

1. When all of her employees are assigned to perform identical routine tasks, a supervisor would PROBABLY find it most difficult to differentiate among these employees as to the
    A. amount of work each completed
    B. initiative each one shows in doing the work
    C. number of errors in each one's work
    D. number of times each one is absent or late

1.____

2. The one of the following guiding principles to which a supervisor should give the GREATEST weight when it becomes necessary to discipline an employee is that the
    A. discipline should be of such a nature as to improve the future work of the employee
    B. main benefit gained in disciplining one employee is that all employees are kept from breaking the same rule
    C. morale of all the employees should be improved by the discipline of the one
    D. rules should be applied in a fixed and unchanging manner

2.____

3. In using praise to encourage employees to do better work, the supervisor should realize that praising an employee too often is not good MAINLY because the
    A. employee will be resented by her fellow employees
    B. employee will begin to think she's doing too much work
    C. praise will lose its value as an incentive
    D. supervisor doesn't have the time to praise an employee frequently

3.____

4. A supervisor notices that one of her best employees has apparently begun to loaf on the job.
In this situation, the supervisor should FIRST
    A. allow the employee a period of grace in view of her excellent record
    B. change the employee's job assignment
    C. determine the reason for the change in the employee's behavior
    D. take disciplinary action immediately as she would with any other employee

4.____

5. A supervisor who wants to get a spirit of friendly cooperation from the employees in her unit is MOST likely to be successful if she
    A. makes no exceptions in strictly enforcing department procedures
    B. shows a cooperative spirit herself
    C. tells them they are the best in the department
    D. treats them to coffee once in a while

5.____

6. *Accidents do not just happen.*   6.___
   In view of this statement, it is important for the super-
   visor to realize that
   A. accidents are sometimes deliberate
   B. combinations of unavoidable circumstances cause
      accidents
   C. she must take the blame for each accident
   D. she should train her employees in accident prevention

7. Suppose your superior points out to you several jobs that   7.___
   were poorly done by the employees under your supervision.
   As the supervisor of these employees, you should
   A. accept responsibility for the poor work and take steps
      to improve the work in the future
   B. blame the employees for shirking on the job while you
      were busy on other work
   C. defend the employees since up to this time they were
      all good workers
   D. explain that the poor work was due to circumstances
      beyond your control

8. If a supervisor discovers a situation which is a possible   8.___
   source of grievance, it would be BEST for her to
   A. be ready to answer the employees when they make a
      direct complaint
   B. do nothing until the employees make a direct complaint
   C. tell the employees, in order to keep them from making
      a direct complaint, that nothing can be done
   D. try to remove the cause before the employees make a
      direct complaint

9. Suppose there is a departmental rule that requires super-   9.___
   visors to prepare reports of unusual incidents by the end
   of the tour of duty in which the incident occurs.
   The MAIN reason for requiring such prompt reporting is that
   A. a quick decision can be made whether the employee
      involved was neglectful of her duty
   B. other required reports cannot be made out until this
      one is turned in
   C. the facts are recorded before they are forgotten or
      confused by those involved in the incident
   D. the report is submitted before the supervisor required
      to make the report may possibly leave the department

10. A GOOD practical method to use in determining whether an   10.___
    employee is doing his job properly is to
    A. assume that if he asks no questions, he knows the work
    B. question him directly on details of the job
    C. inspect and follow-up the work which is assigned to him
    D. ask other employees how this employee is making out

11. If an employee continually asks how he should do his work,   11.___
    you should
    A. dismiss him immediately
    B. pretend you do not hear him unless he persists

C. explain the work carefully but encourage him to use his own judgment
D. tell him not to ask so many questions

12. You have instructed an employee to complete a job in a certain area.
To be sure that the employee understands the instructions you have given him, you should
  A. ask him to repeat the instructions to you
  B. check with him after he has done the job
  C. watch him while he is doing the job
  D. repeat the instructions to the employee

12.____

13. One of your men disagrees with your evaluation of his work.
Of the following, the BEST way to handle this situation would be to
  A. explain that you are in a better position to evaluate his work than he is
  B. tell him that since other men are satisfied with your evaluation, he should accept their opinions
  C. explain the basis of your evaluation and discuss it with him
  D. refuse to discuss his complaint in order to maintain discipline

13.____

14. Of the following, the one which is NOT a quality of leadership desirable in a supervisor is
  A. intelligence   B. integrity
  C. forcefulness   D. partiality

14.____

15. Of the following, the one which LEAST characterizes the grapevine is that it
  A. consists of a tremendous amount of rumor, conjecture, information, advice, prediction, and even orders
  B. seems to rise spontaneously, is largely anonymous, spreads rapidly, and changes in unpredictable directions
  C. can be eliminated without any great effort
  D. commonly fills the gaps left by the regular organizational channels of communication

15.____

16. When a superintendent delegates authority to a foreman, of the following, it would be MOST advisable for the superintendent to
  A. set wide limits of such authority to allow the foreman considerable leeway
  B. define fairly closely the limits of the authority delegated to the foreman
  C. wait until the foreman has some experience in the assignment before setting limits to his authority
  D. inform him that it is the foreman's ultimate basic responsibility to get the work done

16.____

17. One of the hallmarks of a good supervisor is his ability   17.___
    to use many different methods of obtaining information
    about the status of work in progress.
    Which one of the following would *probably* indicate that
    a supervisor does NOT have this ability?
    A. Holding specified staff meetings at specified intervals
    B. Circulating among his subordinates as often as possible
    C. Holding staff meetings only when absolutely necessary
    D. Asking subordinates to come in and discuss the progress
       of their work and their problems

18. Of the following, the one which is the LEAST important   18.___
    factor in deciding that additional training is necessary
    for the men you supervise is that
    A. the quality of work is below standard
    B. supplies are being wasted
    C. too much time is required to do specific jobs
    D. the absentee rate has declined

19. To promote proper safety practices in the operation of   19.___
    power tools and equipment, you should emphasize in meetings
    with the staff that
    A. every accident can be prevented through proper safety
       regulations
    B. proper safety practices will probably make future
       safety meetings unnecessary
    C. when safety rules are followed, tools and equipment
       will work better
    D. safety rules are based on past experience with the
       best methods of preventing accidents

20. Employee morale is the way employees feel about each other   20.___
    and their job.
    To a supervisor, it should be a sign of good morale if the
    employees
    A. are late for work
    B. complain about their work
    C. willingly do difficult jobs
    D. take a long time to do simple jobs

21. A supervisor who encourages his workers to make sugges-   21.___
    tions about job improvement shows his workers that he
    A. is not smart enough to improve the job himself
    B. wants them to take part in making improvements
    C. does not take the job seriously
    D. is not a good supervisor

22. Suppose that your supervisor tells you that a procedure   22.___
    which has been followed for years is going to be changed.
    It is your job to make sure the workers you supervise
    understand and accept the new procedure.
    What would be the BEST thing for you to do in this situation?
    A. Give a copy of the new procedure to each worker with
       orders that it must be followed.
    B. Explain the new procedure to one worker and have him
       explain it to the others.

C. Ask your supervisor to explain the new procedure
   since he has more authority.
D. Call your workers together to explain and discuss the
   new procedure.

23. One of the foundations of scientific management of an   23.___
    organization is the proper use of control measures.
    Of the following, the BEST way, in general, to implement
    control measures is to
       A. develop suitable procedures, systems, and guidelines
          for the organization
       B. evaluate the actual employees' job performance realis-
          tically and reasonably
       C. set standards which are designed to increase produc-
          tivity
       D. publish a set of rules and insist upon strict com-
          pliance with these rules

24. A district superintendent would MOST likely be justified   24.___
    in taking up a matter with his borough superintendent when
    the problem involved
       A. a dispute among different factions in his district
       B. a section foreman's difficulties with his assistant
          foreman
       C. his own men and others not under his control
       D. methods of doing the work and the amount of production

25. The superintendent has the authority to recommend disci-   25.___
    plinary action.
    He can BEST use this authority to
       A. demonstrate his authority as a superintendent
       B. improve a man's work
       C. make it less difficult for other superintendents to
          maintain order
       D. punish the men for wrong-doing

KEY (CORRECT ANSWERS)

1. B		11. C	
2. A		12. A	
3. C		13. C	
4. C		14. D	
5. B		15. C	
6. D		16. B	
7. A		17. B	
8. D		18. D	
9. C		19. D	
10. C		20. C	

21. B
22. D
23. C
24. B
25. B

TEST 2

DIRECTIONS: Each question or incomplete statement is followed by several suggested answers or completions. Select the one that BEST answers the question or completes the statement. *PRINT THE LETTER OF THE CORRECT ANSWER IN THE SPACE AT THE RIGHT.*

1. From the standpoint of equal opportunity, the MOST critical item that a superintendent should focus on is
   A. assigning only minority workers to supervisory positions
   B. helping minority employees to upgrade their knowledge so they may qualify for higher positions
   C. placing minority workers in job categories above their present level of ability so that they can *sink or swim*
   D. disregarding merit system principles

   1.___

2. After careful deliberation, you have decided that one of your workers should be disciplined.
   It is MOST important that the
   A. discipline be severe for best results
   B. discipline be delayed as long as possible
   C. worker understands why he is being disciplined
   D. other workers be consulted before the discipline is administered

   2.___

3. Of the following, the MOST important qualities of an employee chosen for a supervisory position are
   A. education and intelligence
   B. interest in the objectives and activities of the agency
   C. skill in performing the type of work to be supervised
   D. knowledge of the work and leadership ability

   3.___

4. Of the following, the CHIEF characteristic which distinguishes a good supervisor from a poor supervisor is the good supervisor's
   A. ability to favorably impress others
   B. unwillingness to accept monotony or routine
   C. ability to deal constructively with problem situations
   D. strong drive to overcome opposition

   4.___

5. Of the following, the MAIN disadvantage of on-the-job training is that, *generally*,
   A. special equipment may be needed
   B. production may be slowed down
   C. the instructor must maintain an individual relationship with the trainee
   D. the on-the-job instructor must be better qualified than the classroom instructor

   5.___

6. If it becomes necessary for you, as a supervisor, to give   6.___
a subordinate employee confidential information, the MOST
effective of the following steps to take to make sure the
information is kept confidential by the employee is to
      A. tell the employee that the information is confidential
         and is not to be repeated
      B. threaten the employee with disciplinary action if the
         information is repeated
      C. offer the employee a merit increase as an incentive
         for keeping the information confidential
      D. remind the employee at least twice a day that the
         information is confidential and is not to be repeated

7. Three new men have just been assigned to work under your   7.___
supervision. Every time you give them an assignment, one
of these men asks you several questions.
Of the following, the MOST advisable action for you to
take is to
      A. assure him of your confidence in his ability to carry
         out the assignment correctly without asking so many
         questions
      B. have all three men listen to your answers to these
         questions
      C. point out that the other two men do the job without
         asking so many questions
      D. tell him to see if he can get the answers from other
         workers before coming to you

8. Two of your subordinates suggest that you recommend a   8.___
third man for an above-standard service rating because
of his superior work.
You should
      A. ask the two subordinates whether the third man knows
         that they intended to discuss this matter with you
      B. explain to the two subordinates that an above-standard
         service rating for one man would have a detrimental
         effect on many of the other men
      C. recommend the man for an above-standard service rating
         if there is sufficient justification for it
      D. tell the two subordinates that the matter of service
         ratings is not their concern

9. All of the following are indications of good employee   9.___
morale EXCEPT
      A. the number of grievances are lowered
      B. labor turnover is decreased
      C. the amount of supervision required is lowered
      D. levels of production are lowered

10. All of the following statements regarding the issuance of   10.___
direct orders are true EXCEPT
      A. use direct orders only when necessary
      B. make sure that the receiver of the direct order is
         qualified to carry out the order
      C. issue direct orders in clear, concise words
      D. give direct orders only in writing

11. In order to achieve the BEST results in on-the-job training, supervisors should   11.___
    A. allow frequent coffee breaks during the training period
    B. be in a higher salary range than that of the individuals they are training
    C. have had instructions or experience in conducting such training
    D. have had a minimum of five years of experience in the job

12. Of the following, the LEAST important quality of a good supervisor is   12.___
    A. technical competence
    B. teaching ability
    C. ability to communicate with others
    D. ability to socialize with subordinates

13. One of your usually very hard working, reliable employees brings in a bottle of whiskey to celebrate his birthday during the rest period.   13.___
Which one of the following actions should you take?
    A. Offer to pay for the cost of the whiskey
    B. Confiscate the bottle
    C. Tell him to celebrate after working hours
    D. Pretend that you have not seen the bottle of whiskey

14. Assume that you find it necessary to discipline two sub-ordinates, Mr. Tate and Mr. Sawyer, for coming to work late on several occasions. Their latenesses have had disruptive effects on the work schedule, and you have given both of them several verbal warnings. Mr. Tate has been in your work unit for many years, and his work has always been satisfactory. Mr. Sawyer is a probationary employee, who has had some problems in learning your procedures. You decide to give Mr. Tate one more warning, in private, for his latenesses.   14.___
According to good supervisory practice, which one of the following disciplinary actions should you take with regard to Mr. Sawyer?
    A. Give him a reprimand in front of his co-workers, to make a lasting impression.
    B. Recommend dismissal since he has not yet completed his probationary period.
    C. Give him one more warning, in private, for his late-nesses.
    D. Recommend a short suspension or payroll deduction to impress on him the importance of coming to work on time.

15. Assume that you have delegated a very important work assignment to Johnson, one of your most experienced sub-ordinates. Prior to completion of the assignment, your superior accidentally discovers that the assignment is being carried out incorrectly, and tells you about it.   15.___
Which one of the following responses is MOST appropriate for you to give to your superior?
    A. *I take full responsibility, and I will see to it that the assignment is carried out correctly.*

B. *Johnson has been with us for many years now and should know better.*
C. *It really isn't Johnson's fault; rather it is the fault of the ancient equipment we have to do the job.*
D. *I think you should inform Johnson since he is the one at fault, not I.*

16. Assume that you observe that one of your employees is talking excessively with other employees, quitting early, and taking unusually long rest periods. Despite these abuses, she is one of your most productive employees, and her work is usually of the highest quality.
Of the following, the MOST appropriate action to take with regard to this employee is to
    A. ignore these infractions since she is one of your best workers
    B. ask your superior to reprimand her so that you can remain on the employee's good side
    C. reprimand her since not doing so would lower the morale of the other employees
    D. ask another of your subordinates to mention these infractions to the offending employee and suggest that she stop breaking rules

16.____

17. Assume that you have noticed that an employee whose attendance had been quite satisfactory is now showing marked evidence of a consistent pattern of absences.
Of the following, the BEST way to cope with this problem is to
    A. wait several weeks to see whether this pattern continues
    B. meet with the employee to try to find out the reasons for this change
    C. call a staff meeting and discuss the need for good attendance
    D. write a carefully worded warning to the employee

17.____

18. It is generally agreed that the successful supervisor must know how to wisely delegate work to her subordinates since she cannot do everything herself.
Which one of the following practices is MOST likely to result in ineffective delegation by a supervisor?
    A. Establishment of broad controls to assure feedback about any deviations from plans
    B. Willingness to let subordinates use their own ideas about how to get the job done, where appropriate
    C. Constant observance of employees to see if they are making any mistakes
    D. Granting of enough authority to make possible the accomplishment of the delegated work

18.____

19. Suppose that, in accordance with grievance procedures, an employee brings a complaint to you, his immediate supervisor.
In dealing with his complaint, the one of the following which is MOST important for you to do is to
    A. talk to the employee's co-workers to learn whether the complaint is justified

19.____

    B. calm the employee by assuring him that you will look
       into the matter as soon as possible
    C. tell your immediate superior about the employee's
       complaint
    D. give the employee an opportunity to tell the full
       story

20. Holding staff meetings at regular intervals is generally   20.___
    considered to be a good supervisory practice.
    Which one of the following subjects is LEAST desirable
    for discussion at such a meeting?
    A. Revisions in agency personnel policies
    B. Violation of an agency rule by one of the employees
       present
    C. Problems of waste and breakage in the work area
    D. Complaints of employees about working conditions

21. Suppose that you are informed that your staff is soon to   21.___
    be reduced by one-third due to budget problems.
    Which one of the following steps would be LEAST advisable
    in your effort to maintain a quality service with the
    smaller number of employees?
    A. Directing employees to speed up operations
    B. Giving employees training or retraining
    C. Rearranging the work area
    D. Revising work methods

22. Of the following, which action on the part of the super-   22.___
    visor is LEAST likely to contribute to upgrading the
    skills of her subordinates?
    A. Providing appropriate training to subordinates
    B. Making periodic evaluations of subordinates and dis-
       cussing the evaluations with the subordinates
    C. Consistently assigning subordinates to those tasks
       with which they are familiar
    D. Giving increased responsibility to appropriate sub-
       ordinates

23. Suppose that a new employee on your staff has difficulty   23.___
    in performing his assigned tasks after having been given
    training.
    Of the following courses of action, the one which would
    be BEST for you, his supervisor, to take FIRST is to
    A. change his work assignment
    B. give him a poor evaluation since he is obviously
       unable to do the work
    C. give him the training again
    D. have him work with an employee who is more experienced
       in the tasks for a short while

24. Several times, an employee has reported to work unfit for   24.___
    duty because he had been drinking. He refused to get
    counseling for his emotional problems when this was
    suggested by his supervisor. Last week, his supervisor
    warned him that he would face disciplinary action if he
    again reported to work unfit for duty because of drinking.
    Now, the employee has again reported to work in that condition.

Of the following, the BEST action for the supervisor to take now would be to
- A. arrange to have the employee transferred to another work location
- B. give the employee one more chance by pretending to not notice his condition this time
- C. start disciplinary action against the employee
- D. warn him that he will face disciplinary action if he reports for work in that condition again

25. An employee has been calling in sick repeatedly, and these absences have disrupted the work schedule.
To try to make sure that the employee use sick leave only on days when he is actually sick, which of the following actions would be the BEST for his supervisor to take?
- A. Telephone the employee's home on days when he is out on sick leave
- B. Require the employee to obtain a note from a physician explaining the reason for his absence whenever he uses sick leave in the future
- C. Require that he get a complete physical examination and have his doctor send a report to the supervisor
- D. Warn the employee that he will face disciplinary action the next time he stays out on sick leave

25.____

KEY (CORRECT ANSWERS)

1. B		11. C	
2. C		12. D	
3. D		13. C	
4. C		14. C	
5. B		15. A	
6. A		16. C	
7. B		17. B	
8. C		18. C	
9. D		19. D	
10. D		20. B	

21. A
22. C
23. D
24. C
25. B

TEST 3

1. Suppose that, as a supervisor, you have an idea for changing the way a certain task is performed by your staff so that it will be less tedious and get done faster. Of the following, the MOST advisable action for you to take regarding this idea is to
   A. issue a written memorandum explaining the new method and giving reasons why it is to replace the old one
   B. discuss it with your staff to get their reactions and suggestions
   C. set up a training class in the new method for your staff
   D. try it out on an experimental basis on half the staff

1.___

2. A troubled subordinate privately approaches his supervisor in order to talk about a problem on the job. In this situation, the one of the following actions that is NOT desirable on the part of the supervisor is to
   A. ask the subordinate pertinent questions to help develop points further
   B. close his office door during the talk to block noisy distractions
   C. allow sufficient time to complete the discussion with the subordinate
   D. take over the conversation so the employee won't be embarrassed

2.___

3. Suppose that one of your goals as a supervisor is to foster good working relationships between yourself and your employees, without undermining your supervisory effectiveness by being too friendly. Of the following, the BEST way to achieve this goal when dealing with employees' work problems is to
   A. discourage individual personal conferences by using regularly scheduled staff meetings to discuss work problems
   B. try to resolve work problems within a relatively short period of time
   C. insist that employees put all work problems into writing before seeing you
   D. maintain an open-door policy, allowing employees complete freedom of access to you without making appointments to discuss work problems

3.___

4. An employee under your supervision complains that he is   4.___
    assigned to work late more often than any of the other
    employees. You check the records and find that this
    isn't so.
    You should
        A. advise this employee not to worry about what the other
           employees do but to see that he puts in a full day's
           work himself
        B. explain to this employee that you get the same complaint
           from all the other employees
        C. inform this employee that you have checked the records
           and the complaint is not justified
        D. not assign this employee to work late for a few days
           in order to keep him satisfied

5. An employee has reported late for work several times.   5.___
    His supervisor should
        A. give this employee less desirable assignments
        B. overlook the lateness if the employee's work is other-
           wise exceptional
        C. recommend disciplinary action for habitual lateness
        D. talk the matter over with the employee before doing
           anything further

6. In choosing a man to be in charge in his absence, the   6.___
    supervisor should select FIRST the employee who
        A. has ability to supervise others
        B. has been longest with the organization
        C. has the nicest appearance and manner
        D. is most skilled in his assigned duties

7. An employee under your supervision comes to you to complain   7.___
    about a decision you have made in assigning the men. He
    is excited and angry. You think what he is complaining
    about is not important, but it seems very important to him.
    The BEST way for you to handle this is to
        A. let him talk until *he gets it off his chest* and then
           explain the reasons for your decision
        B. refuse to talk to him until he has cooled off
        C. show him at once how unimportant the matter is and
           how ridiculous his arguments are
        D. tell him to take it up with your superior if he
           disagrees with your decision

8. Suppose that a new employee has been appointed and assigned   8.___
    to your supervision.
    When this man reports for work, it would be BEST for you to
        A. ask him questions about different problems connected
           with his line of work and see if he answers them
           correctly
        B. check him carefully while he carries out some routine
           assignment that you give him
        C. explain to him the general nature of the work he will
           be required to do
        D. make a careful study of his previous work record
           before coming to your department

9. *The competent supervisor will be friendly with the*   9.___
   employees under his supervision but will avoid close
   familiarity.
   This statement is justified MAINLY because
   A. a friendly attitude on the part of the supervisor toward
      the employee is likely to cause suspicion on the part of
      the employee
   B. a supervisor can handle his employees better if he
      doesn't know their personal problems
   C. close familiarity may interfere with the discipline
      needed for good supervisor-subordinate relationships
   D. familiarity with the employees may be a sign of lack of
      ability on the part of the supervisor

10. An employee disagrees with the instructions that you, his   10.___
    supervisor, have given him for carrying out a certain
    assignment.
    The BEST action for you to take is to tell this employee
    that
    A. he can do what he wants but you will hold him respon-
       sible for failure
    B. orders must be carried out or morale will fall apart
    C. this job has been done in this way for many years with
       great success
    D. you will be glad to listen to his objections and to
       his suggestions for improvement

11. As a supervisor, it is LEAST important for you to use a   11.___
    new employee's probationary period for the purpose of
    A. carefully checking how he performs the work you
       assign him
    B. determining whether he can perform the duties of his
       job efficiently
    C. preparing him for promotion to a higher position
    D. showing him how to carry out his assigned duties
       properly

12. Suppose you have just given an employee under your super-   12.___
    vision instructions on how to carry out a certain assign-
    ment.
    The BEST way to check that he has understood your instruc-
    tions is to
    A. ask him to repeat your instructions word for word
    B. check the progress of his work the first chance you get
    C. invite him to ask questions if he has any doubts
    D. question him briefly about the main points of the
       assignment

13. Suppose you find it necessary to change a procedure that   13.___
    the men under your supervision have been following for a
    long time.
    A GOOD way to get their cooperation for this change would
    be to
    A. bring them together to talk over the new procedure and
       explain the reasons for its adoption
    B. explain to the men that if most of them still don't
       approve of the change after giving it a fair try, you
       will consider giving it up

C. give them a few weeks' notice of the proposed change in procedure
D. not enforce the new procedure strictly at the beginning

14. An order can be given by a supervisor in such a way as to make the employee want to obey it.
    According to this statement, it is MOST reasonable to suppose that
    A. a person will be glad to obey an order if he realizes that he must
    B. if an order is given properly, it will be obeyed more willingly
    C. it is easier to obey an order than to give one correctly
    D. supervisors should inspire confidence by their actions as well as by their words

14.____

15. If one of the men you supervise disagrees with how you rate his work, the BEST way for you to handle this is to
    A. advise him to appeal to your superior about it
    B. decline to discuss the matter with him in order to keep discipline
    C. explain why you rate him the way you do and talk it over with him
    D. tell him that you are better qualified to rate his work than he is

15.____

16. A supervisor should be familiar with the experience and abilities of the employees under his supervision MAINLY because
    A. each employee's work is highly important and requires a person of outstanding ability
    B. it will help him to know which employees are best fitted for certain assignments
    C. nearly all men have the same basic ability to do any job equally well
    D. superior background shortly shows itself in superior work quality, regardless of assignment

16.____

17. The competent supervisor will try to develop respect rather than fear in his subordinates.
    This statement is justified MAINLY because
    A. fear is always present and, for best results, respect must be developed to offset it
    B. it is generally easier to develop respect in the men than it is to develop fear
    C. men who respect their supervisor are more likely to give more than the required minimum amount and quality of work
    D. respect is based on the individual, and fear is based on the organization as a whole

17.____

18. If one of the employees you supervise does outstanding work, you should   18.___
    A. explain to him how his work can still be improved so that he will not become self-satisfied
    B. mildly criticize the other men for not doing as good a job as this man
    C. praise him for his work so that he will know it is appreciated
    D. say nothing or he might become conceited

19. A supervisor can BEST help establish good morale among his employees if he   19.___
    A. confides in them about his personal problems in order to encourage them to confide in him
    B. encourages them to become friendly with him but discourages social engagements with them
    C. points out to them the advantages of having a coopera-tive spirit in the department
    D. sticks to the same rules that he expects them to follow

20. The one of the following situations which would seem to indicate poor scheduling of work by the supervisor is   20.___
    A. everybody seeming to be very busy at the same time
    B. re-assignment of a man to other work because of breakdown of a piece of equipment
    C. two employees on vacation at the same time
    D. two operators waiting to use the same equipment at the same time

------

KEY (CORRECT ANSWERS)

1.	B	11.	C
2.	D	12.	D
3.	B	13.	A
4.	C	14.	B
5.	D	15.	C
6.	A	16.	B
7.	A	17.	C
8.	C	18.	C
9.	C	19.	D
10.	D	20.	D

PREPARING WRITTEN MATERIAL

PARAGRAPH REARRANGEMENT
COMMENTARY

The sentences which follow are in scrambled order. You are to rearrange them in proper order and indicate the letter choice containing the correct answer at the space at the right.

Each group of sentences in this section is actually a paragraph presented in scrambled order. Each sentence in the group has a place in that paragraph; no sentence is to be left out. You are to read each group of sentences and decide upon the best order in which to put the sentences so as to form as well-organized paragraph.

The questions in this section measure the ability to solve a problem when all the facts relevant to its solution are not given.

More specifically, certain positions of responsibility and authority require the employee to discover connections between events sometimes, apparently, unrelated. In order to do this, the employee will find it necessary to correctly infer that unspecified events have probably occurred or are likely to occur. This ability becomes especially important when action must be taken on incomplete information.

Accordingly, these questions require competitors to choose among several suggested alternatives, each of which presents a different sequential arrangement of the events. Competitors must choose the MOST logical of the suggested sequences.

In order to do so, they may be required to draw on general knowledge to infer missing concepts or events that are essential to sequencing the given events. Competitors should be careful to infer only what is essential to the sequence. The plausibility of the wrong alternatives will always require the inclusion of unlikely events or of additional chains of events which are NOT essential to sequencing the given events.

It's very important to remember that you are looking for the best of the four possible choices, and that the best choice of all may not even be one of the answers you're given to choose from.

There is no one right way to these problems. Many people have found it helpful to first write out the order of the sentences, as they would have arranged them, on their scrap paper before looking at the possible answers. If their optimum answer is there, this can save them some time. If it isn't, this method can still give insight into solving the problem. Others find it most helpful to just go through each of the possible choices, contrasting each as they go along. You should use whatever method feels comfortable, and works, for you.

While most of these types of questions are not that difficult, we've added a higher percentage of the difficult type, just to give you more practice. Usually there are only one or two questions on this section that contain such subtle distinctions that you're unable to answer confidently, and you then may find yourself stuck deciding between two possible choices, neither of which you're sure about.

———

EXAMINATION SECTION
Preparing Written Material

Directions: The following groups of sentences need to be arranged in an order that makes sense. Select the letter preceding the sequence that represents the best sentence order. *PRINT THE LETTER OF THE CORRECT ANSWER IN THE SPACE AT THE RIGHT.*

Group 1

1. _____

1)   The ostrich egg shell's legendary toughness makes it an excellent substitute for certain types of dishes or dinnerware, and in parts of Africa ostrich shells are cut and decorated for use as containers for water.

2)   Since prehistoric times, people have used the enormous egg of the ostrich as a part of their diet, a practice which has required much patience and hard work—to hard-boil an ostrich egg takes about four hours.

3)   Opening the egg's shell, which is rock hard and nearly an inch thick, requires heavy tools, such as a saw or chisel; from inside, a baby ostrich must use a hornlike projection on its beak as a miniature pick-axe to escape from the egg.

4)   The offspring of all higher-order animals originate from single egg cells that are carried by mothers, and most of these eggs are relatively small, often microscopic.

5)   The egg of the African ostrich, however, weighs a massive thirty pounds, making it the largest single cell on earth, and a common object of human curiosity and wonder.

The best order is

A.   5 4 1 2 3
B.   1 4 5 3 2
C.   4 2 3 5 1
D.   4 5 2 3 1

Group 2

1)   Typically only a few feet high on the open sea, individual tsunami have been known to circle the entire globe two or three times if their progress is not interrupted, but are not usually dangerous until they approach the shallow water that surrounds land masses.

2)   Some of the most terrifying and damaging hazards caused by earthquakes are tsunami, which were once called "tidal waves"—a poorly chosen name, since these waves have nothing to do with tides.

3)   Then a wave, slowed by the sudden drag on the lower part of its moving water column, will pile upon itself, sometimes reaching a height of over 100 feet.

4)   Tsunami (Japanese for "great harbor wave") are seismic waves that are caused by earthquakes near oceanic trenches, and once triggered, can travel up to 600 miles an hour on the open ocean.

5)   A land-shoaling tsunami is capable of extraordinary destruction; some tsunami have deposited large boats miles inland, washed out two-foot-thick seawalls, and scattered locomotive trains over long distances.

The best order is

A.   4 1 3 2 5
B.   1 3 4 2 5
C.   5 1 3 2 4
D.   2 4 1 3 5

Group 3

1) Soon, by the 1940's, jazz was the most popular type of music among American intellectuals and college students.

2) In the early days of jazz, it was considered "lowdown" music, or music that was played only in rough, disreputable bars and taverns.

3) However, jazz didn't take long to develop from early ragtime melodies into more complex, sophisticated forms, such as Charlie Parker's "bebop" style of jazz.

4) After charismatic band leaders such as Duke Ellington and Count Basie brought jazz to a larger audience, and jazz continued to evolve into more complicated forms, white audiences began to accept and even to enjoy the new American art form.

5) Many white Americans, who then dictated the tastes of society, were wary of music that was played almost exclusively in black clubs in the poorer sections of cities and towns.

The best order is

A. 5 4 3 2 1
B. 2 5 3 4 1
C. 4 5 3 1 2
D. 1 2 4 3 5

Group 4

1)   Then, hanging in a windless place, the magnetized end of the needle would always point to the south.

2)   The needle could then be balanced on the rim of a cup, or the edge of a fingernail, but this balancing act was hard to maintain, and the needle often fell off.

3)   Other needles would point to the north, and it was important for any traveler finding his way with a compass to remember which kind of magnetized needle he was carrying.

4)   To make some of the earliest compasses in recorded history, ancient Chinese "magicians" would rub a needle with a piece of magnetized iron called a lodestone.

5)   A more effective method of keeping the needle free to swing with its magnetic pull was to attach a strand of silk to the center of the needle with a tiny piece of wax.

The best order is

A.   4 2 5 1 3
B.   4 3 5 2 1
C.   4 5 2 1 3
D.   4 1 3 5 2

Group 5

1)   The now-famous first mate of the *HMS Bounty*, Fletcher Christian, founded one of the world's most peculiar civilizations in 1790.

2)   The men knew they had just committed a crime for which they could be hanged, so they set sail for Pitcairn, a remote, abandoned island in the far eastern region of the Polynesian archipelago, accompanied by twelve Polynesian women and six men.

3)   In a mutiny that has become legendary, Christian and the others forced Captain Bligh into a lifeboat and set him adrift off the coast of Tonga in April of 1789.

4)   In early 1790, the *Bounty* landed at Pitcairn Island, where the men lived out the rest of their lives and founded an isolated community which to this day includes direct descendants of Christian and the other crewmen.

5)   The *Bounty*, commanded by Captain William Bligh, was in the middle of a global voyage, and Christian and his shipmates had come to the conclusion that Bligh was a reckless madman who would lead them to their deaths unless they took the ship from him.

The best order is

A.   4 5 3 2 1
B.   1 3 5 2 4
C.   1 5 3 2 4
D.   3 1 5 4 2

Group 6

1)   But once the vines had been led to make orchids, the flowers had to be carefully hand-pollinated, because unpollinated orchids usually lasted less than a day, wilting and dropping off the vine before it had even become dark.

2)   The Totonac farmers discovered that looping a vine back around once it reached a five-foot height on its host tree would cause the vine to flower.

3)   Though they knew how to process the fruit pods and extract vanilla's flavoring agent, the Totonacs also knew that a wild vanilla vine did not produce abundant flowers or fruit.

4)   Wild vines climbed along the trunks and canopies of trees, and this constant upward growth diverted most of the vine's energy to making leaves instead of the orchid flowers that, once pollinated, would produce the flavorful pods.

5)   Hundreds of years before vanilla became a prized food flavoring in Europe and the Western World, the Totonac Indians of the Mexican Gulf Coast were skilled cultivators of the vanilla vine, whose fruit they literally worshipped as a goddess.

The best order is

A.   2 3 4 1 5
B.   2 4 3 1 5
C.   5 3 4 2 1
D.   3 4 1 2 5

Group 7

1)   Once airborne, the spider is at the mercy of the air currents—usually the spider takes a brief journey, traveling close to the ground, but some have been found in air samples collected as high as 10,000 feet, or been reported landing on ships far out at sea.

2)   Once a young spider has hatched, it must leave the environment into which it was born as quickly as possible, in order to avoid competing with its hundreds of brothers and sisters for food.

3)   The silk rises into warm air currents, and as soon as the pull feels adequate the spider lets go and drifts up into the air, suspended from the silk strand in the same way that a person might parasail.

4)   To help young spiders do this, many species have adapted a practice known as "aerial dispersal," or, in common speech, "ballooning."

5)   A spider that wants to leave its surroundings quickly will climb to the top of a grass stem or twig, face into the wind, and aim its back end into the air, releasing a long stream of silk from the glands near the tip of its abdomen.

The best order is

A.   5 4 2 3 1
B.   5 2 4 1 3
C.   2 5 4 3 1
D.   2 4 5 3 1

Group 8

1)   For about a year, Tycho worked at a castle in Prague with a scientist named Johannes Kepler, but their association was cut short by another argument that drove Kepler out of the castle, to later develop, on his own, the theory of planetary orbits.

2)   Tycho found life without a nose embarrassing, so he made a new nose for himself out of silver, which reportedly remained glued to his face for the rest of his life.

3)   Tycho Brahe, the 17th-century Danish astronomer, is today more famous for his odd and arrogant personality than for any contribution he has made to our knowledge of the stars and planets.

4)   Early in his career, as a student at Rostock University, Tycho got into an argument with the another student about who was the better mathematician, and the two became so angry that the argument turned into a sword fight, during which Tycho's nose was sliced off.

5)   Later in his life, Tycho's arrogance may have kept him from playing a part in one of the greatest astronomical discoveries in history: the elliptical orbits of the solar system's planets.

The best order is

A.   1 4 2 3 5
B.   4 2 3 5 1
C.   4 2 1 3 5
D.   3 4 2 5 1

Group 9

1)   The processionaries are so used to this routine that if a person picks up the end of a silk line and brings it back to the origin—creating a closed circle—the caterpillars may travel around and around for days, sometimes starving ar freezing, without changing course.

2)   Rather than relying on sight or sound, the other caterpillars, who are lined up end-to-end behind the leader, travel to and from their nests by walking on this silk line, and each will reinforce it by laying down its own marking line as it passes over.

3)   In order to insure the safety of individuals, the processionary caterpillar nests in a tree with dozens of other caterpillars, and at night, when it is safest, they all leave together in search of food.

4)   The processionary caterpillar of the European continent is a perfect illustration of how much some insect species rely on instinct in their daily routines.

5)   As they leave their nests, the processionaries form a single-file line behind a leader who spins and lays out a silk line to mark the chosen path.

The best order is

A.   4 3 5 2 1
B.   3 5 4 2 1
C.   3 5 2 1 4
D.   4 5 3 1 2

Group 10

1)   Often, the child is also given a handcrafted walker or push cart, to provide support for its first upright explorations.

2)   In traditional Indian families, a child's first steps are celebrated as a ceremonial event, rooted in ancient myth.

3)   These carts are often intricately designed to resemble the chariot of Krishna, an important figure in Indian mythology.

4)   The sound of these anklet bells is intended to mimic the footsteps of the legendary child Rama, who is celebrated in devotional songs throughout India.

5)   When the child's parents see that the child is ready to begin walking, they will fit it with specially designed ankle bracelets, adorned with gently ringing bells.

The best order is

A.   2 3 4 1 5
B.   2 5 3 1 4
C.   5 4 1 3 2
D.   5 3 2 1 4

Group 11

1)   The settlers planted Osage orange all across Middle America, and today long lines and rectangles of Osage orange trees can still be seen on the prairies, running along the former boundaries of farms that no longer exist.

2)   After trying sod walls and water-filled ditches with no success, American farmers began to look for a plant that was adaptable to prairie weather, and that could be trimmed into a hedge that was "pig-tight, horse-high, and bull-strong."

3)   The tree, so named because it bore a large (but inedible) fruit the size of an orange, was among the sturdiest and hardiest of American trees, and was prized among Native Americans for the strength and flexibility of bows which were made from its wood.

4)   The first people to practice agriculture on the American flatlands were faced with an important problem: what would they use to fence their land in a place that was almost entirely without trees or rocks?

5)   Finally, an Illinois farmer brought the settlers a tree that was native to the land between the Red and Arkansas rivers, a tree called the Osage orange.

The best order is

A.   2 1 5 3 4
B.   1 2 3 4 5
C.   4 2 5 3 1
D.   4 2 1 3 5

Group 12

1) After about ten minutes of such spirited and complicated activity, the head dancer is free to make up his or her own movements while maintaining the interest of the New Year's crowd.

2) The dancer will then perform a series of leg kicks, while at the same time operating the lion's mouth with his own hand and moving the ears and eyes by means of a string which is attached to the dancer's own mouth.

3) The most difficult role of this dance belongs to the one who controls the lion's head; this person must lead all the other "parts" of the lion through the choreographed segments of the dance.

4) The head dancer begins with a complex series of steps, alternately stepping forward with the head raised, and then retreating a few steps while lowering the head, a movement that is intended to create the impression that the lion is keeping a watchful eye for anything evil.

5) When performing a traditional Chinese New Year's lion dance, several performers must fit themselves inside a large lion costume and work together to enact different parts of the dance.

The best order is

A.   5 3 4 2 1
B.   3 4 2 5 1
C.   3 1 5 4 2
D.   4 2 3 5 1

Group 13

1) For many years the shell of the chambered nautilus was treasured in Europe for its beauty and intricacy, but collectors were unaware that they were in possession of the structure that marked a "missing link" in the evolution of marine mollusks.

2) The nautilus, however, evolved a series of enclosed chambers in its shell, and invented a new use for the structure: the shell began to serve as a buoyancy device.

3) Equipped with this new flotation device, the nautilus did not need the single, muscular foot of its predecessors, but instead developed flaps, tentacles, and a gentle form of jet propulsion that transformed it into the first mollusk able to take command of its own destiny and explore a three-dimensional world.

4) By pumping and adjusting air pressure into the chambers, the nautilus could spend the day resting on the bottom, and then rise toward the surface at night in search of food.

5) The nautilus shell looks like a large snail shell, similar to those of its ancestors, who used their shells as protective coverings while they were anchored to the sea floor.

The best order is

A. 5 2 4 1 3
B. 5 1 2 3 4
C. 1 2 5 3 4
D. 1 5 2 4 3

Group 14

1)   While France and England battled for control of the region, the Acadiens prospered on the fertile farmland, which was finally secured by England in 1713.

2)   Early in the 17th century, settlers from western France founded a colony called Acadie in what is now the Canadian province of Nova Scotia.

3)   At this time, English officials feared the presence of spies among the Acadiens who might be loyal to their French homeland, and the Acadiens were deported to spots along the Atlantic and Caribbean shores of America.

4)   The French settlers remained on this land, under English rule, for around forty years, until the beginning of the French and Indian War, another conflict between France and England.

5)   As the Acadien refugees drifted toward a final home in southern Louisiana, neighbors shortened their name to "'Cadien," and finally "Cajun," the name which the descendants of early Acadiens still call themselves.

The best order is

A.   1 4 2 3 5
B.   2 1 3 5 4
C.   2 1 4 3 5
D.   5 2 3 4 1

Group 15

1) Traditional households in the Eastern and Western regions of Africa serve two meals a day—one at around noon, and the other in the evening.

2) The starch is then used in the way that Americans might use a spoon, to scoop up a portion of the main dish on the person's plate.

3) The reason for the starch's inclusion in every meal has to do with taste as well as nutrition; African food can be very spicy, and the starch is known to cool the burning effect of the main dish.

4) When serving these meals, the main dish is usually served on individual plates, and the starch is served on a communal plate, from which diners break off a piece of bread or scoop rice or fufu in their fingers.

5) The typical meals usually consist of a thick stew or soup as the main course, and an accompanying starch—either bread, rice, or *fufu*, a starchy grain paste similar in consistency to mashed potatoes.

The best order is

A.   5 2 3 4 1
B.   5 1 4 3 2
C.   1 4 5 3 2
D.   1 5 4 2 3

1)   In the early days of the American Midwest, Indiana settlers sometimes came together to hold an event called an apple peeling, where neighboring settlers gathered at the homestead of a host family to help prepare the hosts' apple crop for cooking, canning, and making apple butter.

2)   At the beginning of the event, each peeler sat down in front of a ten- or twenty-gallon stone jar and was given a crock of apples and a paring knife.

3)   Once a peeler had finished with a crock, another was placed next to him; if the peeler was an unmarried man, he kept a strict count of the number of apples he had peeled, because the winner was allowed to kiss the girl of his choice.

4)   The peeling usually ended by 9:30 in the evening, when the neighbors gathered in the host family's parlor for a dance social.

5)   The apples were peeled, cored, and quartered, and then placed into the jar.

The best order is

A.   1 5 3 4 2
B.   2 5 3 4 1
C.   1 2 5 3 4
D.   2 1 5 4 3

Group 17

1)   If your pet turtle is a land turtle and is native to temperate climates, it will stop eating some time in October, which should be your cue to prepare the turtle for hibernation.

2)   The box should then be covered with a wire screen, which will protect the turtle from any rodents or predators that might want to take advantage of a motionless and helpless animal.

3)   When your turtle hasn't eaten for a while and appears ready to hibernate, it should be moved to its winter quarters, most likely a cellar or garage, where the temperature should range between 40° and 45°F.

4)   Instead of feeding the turtle, you should bathe it every day in warm water, to encourage the turtle to empty its intestines in preparation for its long winter sleep.

5)   Here the turtle should be placed in a well-ventilated box whose bottom is covered with a moisture-absorbing layer of clay beads, and then filled three-fourths full with almost dry peat moss or wood chips, into which the turtle will burrow and sleep for several months.

The best order is

A.   1 4 3 5 2
B.   3 4 2 5 1
C.   3 2 4 1 5
D.   4 5 2 3 1

1)   Once he has reached the nest, the hunter uses two sturdy bamboo poles like huge chopsticks to pull the nest away from the mountainside, into a large basket that will be lowered to people waiting below.

2)   The world's largest honeybees colonize the Nepalese mountainsides, building honeycombs as large as a person on sheer rock faces that are often hundreds of feet high.

3)   In the remote mountain country of Nepal, a small band of "honey hunt-ers" carry out a tradition so ancient that 10,000 year-old drawings of the practice have been found in the caves of Nepal.

4)   To harvest the honey and beeswax from these combs, a honey hunter climbs above the nests, lowers a long bamboo-fiber ladder over the cliff, and then climbs down.

5)   Throughout this dangerous practice, the hunter is stung repeatedly, and only the veterans, with skin that has been toughened over the years, are able to return from a hunt without the painful swelling caused by stings.

The best order is

A.   2 4 3 5 1
B.   2 4 1 5 3
C.   5 3 2 4 1
D.   3 2 4 1 5

Group 19

1)   After the Romans left Britain, there were relentless attacks on the islands from the barbarian tribes of northern Germany—the Angles, Saxons, and Jutes.

2)   As the empire weakened, Roman soldiers withdrew from Britain, leaving behind a country that continued to practice the Christian religion that had been introduced by the Romans.

3)   Early Latin writings tell of a Christian warrior named Arturius (Arthur, in English) who led the British citizens to defeat these barbarian invaders, and brought an extended period of peace to the lands of Britain.

4)   Long ago, the British Isles were part of the far-flung Roman Empire that extended across most of Europe and into Africa and Asia.

5)   The romantic legend of King Arthur and his knights of the Round Table, one of the most popular and widespread stories of all time, appears to have some foundation in history.

The best order is

A.   5 4 3 2 1
B.   5 4 2 1 3
C.   4 5 2 3 1
D.   4 3 2 1 5

1)   The cylinder was allowed to cool until it sould stand on its own, and then it was cut from the tube and split down the side with a single straight cut.

2)   Nineteenth-century glassmakers, who had not yet discovered the glazier's modern techniques for making panes of glass, had to create a method for converting their blown glass into flat sheets.

3)   The bubble was then pierced at the end to make a hole that opened up while the glassmaker gently spun it, creating a cylinder of glass.

4)   Turned on its side and laid on a conveyor belt, the cylinder was strengthened, or tempered, by being heated again and cooled very slowly, eventually flattening out into a single rectangular piece of glass.

5)   To do this, the glassmaker dipped the end of a long tube into melted glass and blew into the other end of the tube, creating an expanding bubble of glass.

The best order is

A.   2 5 3 4 1
B.   2 4 5 3 1
C.   3 5 2 4 1
D.   3 1 4 5 2

Group 21

1)   The splints are almost always hidden, but horses are occasionally born whose splinted toes project from the leg on either side, just above the hoof.

2)   The second and fourth toes remained, but shrank to thin splints of bone that fused invisibly to the horse's leg bone.

3)   Horses are unique among mammals, having evolved feet that each end in what is essentially a single toe, capped by a large, sturdy hoof.

4)   Julius Caesar, an emperor of ancient Rome, was said to have owned one of these three-toed horses, and considered it so special that he would not permit anyone else to ride it.

5)   Though the horse's earlier ancestors possessed the traditional mammalian set of five toes on each foot, the horse has retained only its third toe; its first and fifth toes disappeared completely as the horse evolved.

The best order is

A.   3 5 2 1 4
B.   5 3 2 4 1
C.   3 2 5 1 4
D.   5 2 3 1 4

1)   The new building materials—some of which are twenty feet long, and weigh nearly six tons—were transported to Pohnpei on rafts, and were brought into their present position by using hibiscus fiber ropes and leverage to move the stone columns upward along the inclined trunks of coconut palm trees.

2)   The ancestors built great fires to heat the stone, and then poured cool seawater on the columns, which caused the stone to contract and split along natural fracture lines.

3)   The now-abandoned enclave of Nan Madol, a group of 92 man-made islands off the shore of the Micronesian island of Pohnpei, is estimated to have been built around the year 500 A.D.

4)   The islanders say their ancestors quarried stone columns from a nearby island, where large basalt columns were formed by the cooling of molten lava.

5)   The structures of Nan Madol are remarkable for the sheer size of some of the stone "logs" or columns that were used to create the walls of the off-shore community, and today anthropologists can only rely on the information of existing local people for clues about how Nan Madol was built.

The best order is

A.   5 4 3 2 1
B.   5 3 1 4 2
C.   3 5 4 2 1
D.   3 1 4 2 5

Group 23

1)   One of the most easily manipulated substances on earth, glass can be made into ceramic tiles that are composed of over 90% air.

2)   NASA's space shuttles are the first spacecraft ever designed to leave and re-enter the earth's atmosphere while remaining intact.

3)   These ceramic tiles are such effective insulators that when a tile emerges from the oven in which it was fired, it can be held safely in a person's hand by the edges while its interior still glows at a temperature well over 2000° F.

4)   Eventually, the engineers were led to a material that is as old as our most ancient civilizations—glass.

5)   Because the temperature during atmospheric re-entry is so incredibly hot, it took NASA's engineers some time to find a substance capable of protecting the shuttles.

The best order is

A.   5 2 1 3 4
B.   2 5 4 1 3
C.   2 3 1 2 5
D.   5 4 3 1 2

Group 24

1)   The secret to teaching any parakeet to talk is patience, and the under-standing that when a bird "talks," it is simply imitating what it hears, rather than putting ideas into words.

2)   You should stay just out of sight of the bird and repeat the phrase you want it to learn, for at least fifteen minutes every morning and evening.

3)   It is important to leave the bird without any words of encouragement or farewell; otherwise it might combine stray remarks or phrases, such as "Good night," with the phrase you are trying to teach it.

4)   For this reason, to train your bird to imitate your words you should keep it free of any distractions, especially other noises, while you are giving it "lessons."

5)   After your repetition, you should quietly leave the bird alone for a while, to think over what it has just heard.

The best order is

A.   1 4 2 5 3
B.   1 2 4 3 5
C.   3 2 1 5 4
D.   3 1 5 4 2

Group 25

1) As a school approaches, fishermen from neighboring communities join their fishing boats together as a fleet, and string their gill nets together to make a huge fence that is held up by cork floats.

2) At a signal from the party leaders, or *nakura*, the family members pound the sides of the boats or beat the water with long poles, creating a sudden and deafening noise.

3) The fishermen work together to drag the trap into a half-circle that may reach 300 yards in diameter, and then the families move their boats to form the other half of the circle around the school of fish.

4) The school of fish flee from the commotion into the awaiting trap, where a final wall of net is thrown over the open end of the half-circle, securing the day's haul.

5) Indonesian people from the area around the Sulu islands live on the sea, in floating villages made of lashed-together or stilted homes, and make much of their living by fishing their home waters for migrating schools of snapper, scad, and other fish.

The best order is

A. 1 5 3 4 2
B. 1 2 4 3 5
C. 5 1 2 3 4
D. 5 1 3 2 4

KEY (CORRECT ANSWERS)

1. D
2. D
3. B
4. A
5. C

6. C
7. D
8. D
9. A
10. B

11. C
12. A
13. D
14. C
15. D

16. C
17. A
18. D
19. B
20. A

21. A
22. C
23. B
24. A
25. D

PHILOSOPHY, PRINCIPLES, PRACTICES, AND TECHNICS
OF
SUPERVISION, ADMINISTRATION, MANAGEMENT, AND ORGANIZATION
CONTENTS

CONTENTS (cont'd)

PHILOSOPHY, PRINCIPLES, PRACTICES, AND TECHNICS
OF
SUPERVISION, ADMINISTRATION, MANAGEMENT, AND ORGANIZATION

I. MEANING OF SUPERVISION

The extension of the democratic philosophy has been accompanied by an extension in the scope of supervision. Modern leaders and supervisors no longer think of supervision in the narrow sense of being confined chiefly to visiting employees, supplying materials, or rating the staff. They regard supervision as being intimately related to all the concerned agencies of society, they speak of the supervisor's function in terms of "growth", rather than the "improvement," of employees

This modern concept of supervision may be defined as follows:

Supervision is leadership and the development of leadership within groups which are cooperatively engaged in inspection, research, training, guidance and evaluation.

II. THE OLD AND THE NEW SUPERVISION

TRADITIONAL	*MODERN*
1. Inspection	1. Study and analysis
2. Focused on the employee	2. Focused on aims, materials, methods, supervisors, employees, environment
3. Visitation	3. Demonstrations, intervisitation, workshops, directed reading, bulletins, etc.
4. Random and haphazard	4. Definitely organized and planned (scientific)
5. Imposed and authoritarian	5. Cooperative and democratic
6. One person usually	6. Many persons involved (creative)

III. THE EIGHT (8) BASIC PRINCIPLES OF THE NEW SUPERVISION

1. *PRINCIPLE OF RESPONSIBILITY*

   Authority to act and responsibility for acting must be joined.

   a. If you give responsibility, give authority.
   b. Define employee duties clearly.
   c. Protect employees from criticism by others.
   d. Recognize the rights as well as obligations of employees.
   e. Achieve the aims of a democratic society insofar as it is possible within the area of your work.
   f. Establish a situation favorable to training and learning.
   g. Accept ultimate responsibility for everything done in your section, unit, office, division, department.
   h. Good administration and good supervision are inseparable.

2. *PRINCIPLE OF AUTHORITY*

   The success of the supervisor is measured by the extent to which the power of authority is not used.

   a. Exercise simplicity and informality in supervision.
   b. Use the simplest machinery of supervision.
   c. If it is good for the organization as a whole, it is probably justified.
   d. Seldom be arbitrary or authoritative.
   e. Do not base your work on the power of position or of personality.
   f. Permit and encourage the free expression of opinions.

3. *PRINCIPLE OF SELF-GROWTH*

   The success of the supervisor is measured by the extent to which, and the speed with which, he is no longer needed.

   a. Base criticism on principles, not on specifics.
   b. Point out higher activities to employees.

    c. Train for self-thinking by employees,to meet new situations.
    d. Stimulate initiative,self-reliance and individual responsibility.
    e. Concentrate on stimulating the growth of employees rather than
       on removing defects.
4. *PRINCIPLE OF INDIVIDUAL WORTH*
   Respect for the individual is a paramount consideration in supervision.
    a. Be human and sympathetic in dealing with employees.
    b. Don't nag about things to be done.
    c. Recognize the individual differences among employees and seek
       opportunities to permit best expression of each personality.
5. *PRINCIPLE OF CREATIVE LEADERSHIP*
   The best supervision is that which is not apparent to the employee.
    a. Stimulate,don't drive employees to creative action.
    b. Emphasize doing good things.
    c. Encourage employees to do what they do best.
    d. Do not be too greatly concerned with details of subject or
       method.
    e. Do not be concerned exclusively with immediate problems and
       activities.
    f. Reveal higher activities and make them both desired and maxi-
       mally possible.
    g. Determine procedures in the light of each situation but see
       that these are derived from a sound basic philosophy.
    h. Aid, inspire and lead so as to liberate the creative spirit
       latent in all good employees.
6. *PRINCIPLE OF SUCCESS AND FAILURE*
   There are no unsuccessful employees, only unsuccessful supervisors
  who have failed to give proper leadership.
    a. Adapt suggestions to the capacities, attitudes, and prejudices
       of employees.
    b. Be gradual, be progressive, be persistent.
    c. Help the employee find the general principle; have the employee
       apply his own problem to the general principle.
    d. Give adequate appreciation for good work and honest effort.
    e. Anticipate employee difficulties and help to prevent them.
    f. Encourage employees to do the desirable things they will do
       anyway.
    g. Judge your supervision by the results it secures.
7. *PRINCIPLE OF SCIENCE*
   Successful supervision is scientific,objective,and experimental.
  It is based on facts, not on prejudices.
    a. Be cumulative in results.
    b. Never divorce your suggestions from the goals of training.
    c. Don't be impatient of results.
    d. Keep all matters on a professional, not a personal level.
    e. Do not be concerned exclusively with immediate problems and
       activities.
    f. Use objective means of determining achievement and rating.
       where possible.
8. *PRINCIPLE OF COOPERATION*
   Supervision is a cooperative enterprise between supervisor
  and employee.
    a. Begin with conditions as they are.
    b. Ask opinions of all involved when formulating policies.

    c. Organization is as good as its weakest link.
    d. Let employees help to determine policies and department
       programs.
    e. Be approachable and accessible - physically and mentally.
    f. Develop pleasant social relationships.
IV. WHAT IS ADMINISTRATION?
    Administration is concerned with providing the environment, the
material facilities, and the operational procedures that will promote
the maximum growth and development of supervisors and employees. (Organization is an aspect, and a concomitant, of administration.)
    There is no sharp line of demarcation between supervision and ad-
ministration; these functions are intimately interrelated and, often,
overlapping. They are complementary activities.
    1. *PRACTICES COMMONLY CLASSED AS "SUPERVISORY"*
        a. Conducting employees conferences
        b. Visiting sections, units, offices, divisions, departments
        c. Arranging for demonstrations
        d. Examining plans
        e. Suggesting professional reading
        f. Interpreting bulletins
        g. Recommending in-service training courses
        h. Encouraging experimentation
        i. Appraising employee morale
        j. Providing for intervisitation
    2. *PRACTICES COMMONLY CLASSIFIED AS "ADMINISTRATIVE"*
        a. Management of the office
        b. Arrangement of schedules for extra duties
        c. Assignment of rooms or areas
        d. Distribution of supplies
        e. Keeping records and reports
        f. Care of audio-visual materials
        g. Keeping inventory records
        h. Checking record cards and books
        i. Programming special activities
        j. Checking on the attendance and punctuality of employees
    3. *PRACTICES COMMONLY CLASSIFIED AS BOTH "SUPERVISORY" AND
       "ADMINISTRATIVE"*
        a. Program construction
        b. Testing or evaluating outcomes
        c. Personnel accounting
        d. Ordering instructional materials
V. RESPONSIBILITIES OF THE SUPERVISOR
    A person employed in a supervisory capacity must constantly be
able to improve his own efficiency and ability. He represents the
employer to the employees and only continuous self-examination can
make him a capable supervisor.
    Leadership and training are the supervisor's responsibility. An
efficient working unit is one in which the employees work with the
supervisor. It is his job to bring out the best in his employees.
He must always be relaxed, courteous and calm in his association with
his employees. Their feelings are important, and a harsh attitude
does not develop the most efficient employees.

3

VI. COMPETENCIES OF THE SUPERVISOR
   1. Complete knowledge of the duties and responsibilities of his position.
   2. To be able to organize a job, plan ahead and carry through.
   3. To have self-confidence and initiative.
   4. To be able to handle the unexpected situation and make quick decisions.
   5. To be able to properly train subordinates in the positions they are best suited for.
   6. To be able to keep good human relations among his subordinates.
   7. To be able to keep good human relations between his subordinates and himself and to earn their respect and trust.

VII. THE PROFESSIONAL SUPERVISOR-EMPLOYEE RELATIONSHIP

There are two kinds of efficiency: one kind is only apparent and is produced in organizations through the exercise of mere discipline; this is but a simulation of the second, or true, efficiency which springs from spontaneous cooperation. If you are a manager, no matter how great or small your responsibility, it is your job, in the final analysis, to create and develop this involuntary cooperation among the people whom you supervise. For, no matter how powerful a combination of money, machines, and materials a company may have, this is a dead and sterile thing without a team of willing, thinking and articulate people to guide it.

The following 21 points are presented as indicative of the exemplary basic relationship that should exist between supervisor and employee:

   1. Each person wants to be liked and respected by his fellow employee and wants to be treated with consideration and respect by his superior.
   2. The most competent employee will make an error. However, in a unit where good relations exist between the supervisor and his employees, tenseness and fear do not exist. Thus, errors are not hidden or covered up and the efficiency of a unit is not impaired.
   3. Subordinates resent rules, regulations, or orders that are unreasonable or unexplained.
   4. Subordinates are quick to resent unfairness, harshness, injustices and favoritism.
   5. An employee will accept responsibility if he knows that he will be complimented for a job well done, and not too harshly chastized for failure; that his supervisor will check the cause of the failure, and, if it was the supervisor's fault, he will assume the blame therefor. If it was the employee's fault, his supervisor will explain the correct method or means of handling the responsibility.
   6. An employee wants to receive credit for a suggestion he has made, that is used. If a suggestion cannot be used, the employee is entitled to an explanation. The supervisor should not say "no" and close the subject.
   7. Fear and worry slow up a worker's ability. Poor working environment can impair his physical and mental health. A good supervisor avoids forceful methods, threats and arguments to get a job done.
   8. A forceful supervisor is able to train his employees individually and as a team, and is able to motivate them in the proper channels.

4

9. A mature supervisor is able to properly evaluate his subordinates and to keep them happy and satisfied.
10. A sensitive supervisor will never patronize his subordinates.
11. A worthy supervisor will respect his employees' confidences.
12. Definite and clear-cut responsibilities should be assigned to each executive.
13. Responsibility should always be coupled with corresponding authority.
14. No change should be made in the scope or responsibilities of a position without a definite understanding to that effect on the part of all persons concerned.
15. No executive or employee, occupying a single position in the organization, should be subject to definite orders from more than one source.
16. Orders should never be given to subordinates over the head of a responsible executive. Rather than do this, the officer in question should be supplanted.
17. Criticisms of subordinates should, whever possible, be made privately, and in no case should a subordinate be criticized in the presence of executives or employees of equal or lower rank.
18. No dispute or difference between executives or employees as to authority or responsibilities should be considered too trivial for prompt and careful adjudication.
19. Promotions, wage changes, and disciplinary action should always be approved by the executive immediately superior to the one directly responsible.
20. No executive or employee should ever be required, or expected, to be at the same time an assistant to, and critic of, another.
21. Any executive whose work is subject to regular inspection should, whever practicable, be given the assistance and facilities necessary to enable him to maintain an independent check of the quality of his work.

VIII. MINI-TEXT IN SUPERVISION, ADMINISTRATION, MANAGEMENT, AND ORGANIZATION
A. BRIEF HIGHLIGHTS

Listed concisely and sequentially are major headings and important data in the field for quick recall and review.

1. *LEVELS OF MANAGEMENT*

Any organization of some size has several levels of management. In terms of a ladder the levels are:

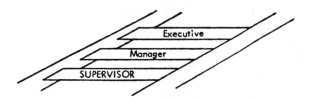

The first level is very important because it is the beginning point of management leadership.

2. *WHAT THE SUPERVISOR MUST LEARN*

A supervisor must learn to:
    (1) Deal with people and their differences
    (2) Get the job done through people
    (3) Recognize the problems when they exist
    (4) Overcome obstacles to good performance
    (5) Evaluate the performance of people
    (6) Check his own performance in terms of accomplishment

3. *A DEFINITION OF SUPERVISOR*
   The term supervisor means any individual having authority, in the interests of the employer, to hire, transfer, suspend, lay-off, recall, promote, discharge, assign, reward, or discipline other employees... or responsibility to direct them, or to adjust their grievances, or effectively to recommend such action, if, in connection with the foregoing, exercise of such authority is not of a merely routine or clerical nature but requires the use of independent judgment.

4. *ELEMENTS OF THE TEAM CONCEPT*
   What is involved in teamwork? The component parts are:

   (1) Members   (3) Goals   (5) Cooperation
   (2) A leader   (4) Plans   (6) Spirit

5. *PRINCIPLES OF ORGANIZATION*
   (1) A team member must know what his job is
   (2) Be sure that the nature and scope of a job are understood
   (3) Authority and responsibility should be carefully spelled out
   (4) A supervisor should be permitted to make the maximum number of decisions affecting his employees
   (5) Employees should report to only one supervisor
   (6) A supervisor should direct only as many employees as he can handle effectively
   (7) An organization plan should be flexible
   (8) Inspection and performance of work should be separate
   (9) Organizational problems should receive immediate attention
   (10) Assign work in line with ability and experience

6. *THE FOUR IMPORTANT PARTS OF EVERY JOB*
   (1) Inherent in every job is the *accountability* for results
   (2) A second set of factors in every job are *responsibilities*
   (3) Along with duties and responsibilities one must have the *authority* to act within certain limits without obtaining permission to proceed
   (4) No job exists in a vacuum. The supervisor is surrounded by key *relationships*

7. *PRINCIPLES OF DELEGATION*
   Where work is delegated for the first time, the supervisor should think in terms of these questions:
   (1) Who is best qualified to do this?
   (2) Can an employee improve his abilities by doing this?
   (3) How long should an employee spend on this?
   (4) Are there any special problems for which he will need guidance?
   (5) How broad a delegation can I make?

8. *PRINCIPLES OF EFFECTIVE COMMUNICATIONS*
   (1) Determine the media
   (2) To whom directed?
   (3) Identification and source authority
   (4) Is communication understood?

9. *PRINCIPLES OF WORK IMPROVEMENT*
   (1) Most people usually do only the work which is assigned to them
   (2) Workers are likely to fit assigned work into the time available to perform it
   (3) A good workload usually stimulates output
   (4) People usually do their best work when they know that results will be reviewed or inspected

      (5) Employees usually feel that someone else is responsible for conditions of work, workplace layout, job methods, type of tools and equipment, and other such factors

      (6) Employees are usually defensive about their job security

      (7) Employees have natural resistance to change

      (8) Employees can support or destroy a supervisor

      (9) A supervisor usually earns the respect of his people through his personal example of diligence and efficiency

10. AREAS OF JOB IMPROVEMENT

The *areas* of job improvement are quite numerous, but the most common ones which a supervisor can identify and utilize are:

(1) Departmental layout   (5) Work methods
(2) Flow of work   (6) Materials handling
(3) Workplace layout   (7) Utilization
(4) Utilization of manpower   (8) Motion economy

11. SEVEN KEY POINTS IN MAKING IMPROVEMENTS

(1) Select the job to be improved
(2) Study how it is being done now
(3) Question the present method
(4) Determine actions to be taken
(5) Chart proposed method
(6) Get approval and apply
(7) Solicit worker participation

12. CORRECTIVE TECHNIQUES OF JOB IMPROVEMENT

Specific Problems	General Problems	Corrective Technique
(1) Size of workload	(1) Departmental layout	(1) Study with scale model
(2) Inability to meet schedules	(2) Flow of work	(2) Flow chart study
(3) Strain and fatigue	(3) Workplan layout	(3) Motion analysis
(4) Improper use of men and skills	(4) Utilization of manpower	(4) Comparison of units produced to standard allowances
(5) Waste, poor quality, unsafe conditions	(5) Work methods	(5) Methods analysis
(6) Bottleneck conditions that hinder output	(6) Materials handling	(6) Flow chart and equipment study
(7) Poor utilization of equipment and machines	(7) Utilization of equipment	(7) Down time vs. running time
(8) Efficiency and productivity of labor	(8) Motion economy	(8) Motion analysis

13. A PLANNING CHECKLIST

(1) Objectives   (8) Equipment
(2) Controls   (9) Supplies and materials
(3) Delegations   (10) Utilization of time
(4) Communications   (11) Safety
(5) Resources   (12) Money
(6) Methods and procedures   (13) Work
(7) Manpower   (14) Timing of improvements

14. FIVE CHARACTERISTICS OF GOOD DIRECTIONS

In order to get results, directions must be:

(1) Possible of accomplishment   (4) Planned and complete
(2) Agreeable with worker interests   (5) Unmistakably clear
(3) Related to mission

15. *TYPES OF DIRECTIONS*
        (1) Demands or direct orders   (3) Suggestion or implication
        (2) Requests   (4) Volunteering

16. *CONTROLS*
    A typical listing of the overall areas in which the supervisor should establish controls might be:
        (1) Manpower   (4) Quantity of work   (7) Money
        (2) Materials   (5) Time   (8) Methods
        (3) Quality of work (6) Space

17. *ORIENTING THE NEW EMPLOYEE*
        (1) Prepare for him   (3) Orientation for the job
        (2) Welcome the new employee (4) Follow-up

18. *CHECKLIST FOR ORIENTING NEW EMPLOYEES*

		Yes	*No*
(1)	Do your appreciate the feelings of new employees when they first report for work?	...	...
(2)	Are you aware of the fact that the new employee must make a big adjustment to his job?	...	...
(3)	Have you given him good reasons for liking the job and the organization?	...	...
(4)	Have you prepared for his first day on the job?	...	...
(5)	Did you welcome him cordially and make him feel needed?	...	...
(6)	Did you establish rapport with him so that he feels free to talk and discuss matters with you?	...	...
(7)	Did you explain his job to him and his relationship to you?	...	...
(8)	Does he know that his work will be evaluated periodically on a basis that is fair and objective?	...	...
(9)	Did you introduce him to his fellow workers in such a way that they are likely to accept him?	...	...
(10)	Does he know what employee benefits he will receive?	...	...
(11)	Does he understand the importance of being on the job and what to do if he must leave his duty station?	...	...
(12)	Has he been impressed with the importance of accident prevention and safe practice?	...	...
(13)	Does he generally know his way around the department?	...	...
(14)	Is he under the guidance of a sponsor who will teach the right ways of doing things?	...	...
(15)	Do you plan to follow-up so that he will continue to adjust successfully to his job?	...	...

19. *PRINCIPLES OF LEARNING*
        (1) Motivation (2) Demonstration or explanation
        (3) Practice

20. *CAUSES OF POOR PERFORMANCE*
        (1) Improper training for job   (6) Lack of standards of
        (2) Wrong tools   performance
        (3) Inadequate directions   (7) Wrong work habits
        (4) Lack of supervisory follow-up(8) Low morale
        (5) Poor communications   (9) Other

21. *FOUR MAJOR STEPS IN ON-THE-JOB INSTRUCTION*
        (1) Prepare the worker   (3) Tryout performance
        (2) Present the operation   (4) Follow-up

22. *EMPLOYEES WANT FIVE THINGS*
   (1) Security (2) Opportunity (3) Recognition
   (4) Inclusion (5) Expression
23. *SOME DON'TS IN REGARD TO PRAISE*
   (1) Don't praise a person for something he hasn't done
   (2) Don't praise a person unless you can be sincere
   (3) Don't be sparing in praise just because your superior
       withholds it from you
   (4) Don't let too much time elapse between good performance
       and recognition of it
24. *HOW TO GAIN YOUR WORKERS' CONFIDENCE*
   Methods of developing confidence include such things as:
   (1) Knowing the interests, habits, hobbies of employees
   (2) Admitting your own inadequacies
   (3) Sharing and telling of confidence in others
   (4) Supporting people when they are in trouble
   (5) Delegating matters that can be well handled
   (6) Being frank and straightforward about problems and work-
       ing conditions
   (7) Encouraging others to bring their problems to you
   (8) Taking action on problems which impede worker progress
25. *SOURCES OF EMPLOYEE PROBLEMS*
   On-the-job causes might be such things as:
   (1) A feeling that favoritism is exercised in assignments
   (2) Assignment of overtime
   (3) An undue amount of supervision
   (4) Changing methods or systems
   (5) Stealing of ideas or trade secrets
   (6) Lack of interest in job
   (7) Threat of reduction in force
   (8) Ignorance or lack of communications
   (9) Poor equipment
   (10) Lack of knowing how supervisor feels toward employee
   (11) Shift assignments
   Off-the-job problems might have to do with:
   (1) Health (2) Finances (3) Housing (4) Family
26. *THE SUPERVISOR'S KEY TO DISCIPLINE*
   There are several key points about discipline which the supervisor should keep in mind:
   (1) Job discipline is one of the disciplines of life and is
       directed by the supervisor.
   (2) It is more important to correct an employee fault than to
       fix blame for it.
   (3) Employee performance is affected by problems both on the
       job and off.
   (4) Sudden or abrupt changes in behavior can be indications of
       important employee problems.
   (5) Problems should be dealt with as soon as possible after
       they are identified.
   (6) The attitude of the supervisor may have more to do with
       solving problems than the techniques of problem solving.
   (7) Correction of employee behavior should be resorted to only
       after the supervisor is sure that training or counseling
       will not be helpful
   (8) Be sure to document your disciplinary actions.

(9) Make sure that you are disciplining on the basis of facts rather than personal feelings.

(10) Take each disciplinary step in order, being careful not to make snap judgments, or decisions based on impatience.

27. *FIVE IMPORTANT PROCESSES OF MANAGEMENT*
   (1) Planning   (2) Organizing   (3) Scheduling
   (4) Controlling   (5) Motivating

28. *WHEN THE SUPERVISOR FAILS TO PLAN*
   (1) Supervisor creates impression of not knowing his job
   (2) May lead to excessive overtime
   (3) Job runs itself-- supervisor lacks control
   (4) Deadlines and appointments missed
   (5) Parts of the work go undone
   (6) Work interrupted by emergencies
   (7) Sets a bad example
   (8) Uneven workload creates peaks and valleys
   (9) Too much time on minor details at expense of more important tasks

29. *FOURTEEN GENERAL PRINCIPLES OF MANAGEMENT*
   (1) Division of work
   (2) Authority and responsibility
   (3) Discipline
   (4) Unity of command
   (5) Unity of direction
   (6) Subordination of individual interest to general interest
   (7) Remuneration of personnel
   (8) Centralization
   (9) Scalar chain
   (10) Order
   (11) Equity
   (12) Stability of tenure of personnel
   (13) Initiative
   (14) Esprit de corps

30. *CHANGE*

Bringing about change is perhaps attempted more often, and yet less well understood, than anything else the supervisor does. How do people generally react to change? (People tend to resist change that is imposed upon them by other individuals or circumstances.)

Change is characteristic of every situation. It is a part of **every** real endeavor where the efforts of people are concerned.

A. Why do people resist change?
   People may resist change because of:
      (1) Fear of the unknown
      (2) Implied criticism
      (3) Unpleasant experiences in the past
      (4) Fear of loss of status
      (5) Threat to the ego
      (6) Fear of loss of economic stability

B. How can we best overcome the resistance to change?
   In initiating change, take these steps:
      (1) Get ready to sell
      (2) identify sources of help
      (3) Anticipate objections
      (4) Sell benefits
      (5) Listen in depth
      (6) Follow up

B. BRIEF TOPICAL SUMMARIES

I. WHO/WHAT IS THE SUPERVISOR?
1. The supervisor is often called the "highest level employee and the lowest level manager."
2. A supervisor is a member of both management and the work group. He acts as a bridge between the two.
3. Most problems in supervision are in the area of human relations, or people problems.
4. Employees expect: Respect, opportunity to learn and to advance, and a sense of belonging, and so forth.
5. Supervisors are responsible for directing people and organizing work. Planning is of paramount importance.
6. A position description is a set of duties and responsibilities inherent to a given position.
7. It is important to keep the position description up-to-date and to provide each employee with his own copy.

II. THE SOCIOLOGY OF WORK
1. People are alike in many ways; however each individual is unique.
2. The supervisor is challenged in getting to know employee differences. Acquiring skills in evaluating individuals is an asset.
3. Maintaining meaningful working relationships in the organization is of great importance.
4. The supervisor has an obligation to help individuals to develop to their fullest potential.
5. Job rotation on a planned basis helps to build versatility and to maintain interest and enthusiasm in work groups.
6. Cross training (job rotation) provides backup skills.
7. The supervisor can help reduce tension by maintaining a sense of humor, providing guidance to employees, and by making reasonable and timely decisions. Employees respond favorably to working under reasonably predictable circumstances.
8. Change is characteristic of all managerial behavior. The supervisor must adjust to changes in procedures, new methods, technological changes, and to a number of new and sometimes challenging situations.
9. To overcome the natural tendency for people to resist change, the supervisor should become more skillful in initiating change.

III. PRINCIPLES AND PRACTICES OF SUPERVISION
1. Employees should be required to answer to only one superior.
2. A supervisor can effectively direct only a limited number of employees, depending upon the complexity, variety, and proximity of the jobs involved.
3. The organizational chart presents the organization in graphic form. It reflects lines of authority and responsibility as well as inter-relationships of units within the organization.
4. Distribution of work can be improved through an analysis using the "Work Distribution Chart."
5. The "Work Distribution Chart" reflects the division of work within a unit in understandable form.
6. When related tasks are given to an employee, he has a better chance of increasing his skills through training.
7. The individual who is given the responsibility for tasks must also be given the appropriate authority to insure adequate results.
8. The supervisor should delegate repetitive, routine work. Preparation of recurring reports, maintaining leave and attendance records are some examples.

9. Good discipline is essential to good task performance. Discipline is reflected in the actions of employees on the job in the absence of supervision.

10. Disciplinary action may have to be taken when the positive aspects of discipline have failed. Reprimand,warning,and suspension are examples of disciplinary action.

11. If a situation calls for a reprimand, be sure it is deserved and remember it is to be done in private.

IV. DYNAMIC LEADERSHIP

1. A style is a personal method or manner of exerting influence.

2. Authoritarian leaders often see themselves as the source of power and authority.

3. The democratic leader often perceives the group as the source of authority and power.

4. Supervisors tend to do better when using the pattern of leadership that is most natural for them.

5. Social scientists suggest that the effective supervisor use the leadership style that best fits the problem or circumstances involved.

6. All four styles -- telling,selling,consulting,joining -- have their place. Using one does not preclude using the other at another time.

7. The theory X point of view assumes that the average person dislikes work, will avoid it whenever possible, and must be coerced to achieve organizational objectives.

8. The theory Y point of view assumes that the average person considers work to be as natural as play, and,when the individual is committed, he requires little supervision or direction to accomplish desired objectives.

9. The leader's basic assumptions concerning human behavior and human nature affect his actions, decisions, and other managerial practices.

10. Dissatisfaction among employees is often present,but difficult to isolate. The supervisor should seek to weaken dissatisfaction by keeping promises,being sincere and considerate, keeping employees informed, and so forth.

11. Constructive suggestions should be encouraged during the natural progress of the work.

V. PROCESSES FOR SOLVING PROBLEMS

1. People find their daily tasks more meaningful and satisfying when they can improve them.

2. The causes of problems,or the key factors,are often hidden in the background. Ability to solve problems often involves the ability to isolate them from their backgrounds. There is some substance to the cliché that some persons "can't see the forest for the trees."

3. New procedures are often developed from old ones. Problems should be broken down into manageable parts. New ideas can be adapted from old ones.

4. People think differently in problem-solving situations. Using a logical,patterned approach is often useful. One approach found to be useful includes these steps:
   (a) Define the problem   (d) Weigh and decide
   (b) Establish objectives   (e) Take action
   (c) Get the facts   (f) Evaluate action

VI. TRAINING FOR RESULTS

1. Participants respond best when they feel training is important to them.
2. The supervisor has responsibility for the training and development of those who report to him.
3. When training is delegated to others, great care must be exercised to insure the trainer has knowledge, aptitude, and interest for his work as a trainer.
4. Training (learning) of some type goes on continually. The most successful supervisor makes certain the learning contributes in a productive manner to operational goals.
5. New employees are particularly susceptible to training. Older employees facing new job situations require specific training, as well as having need for development and growth opportunities.
6. Training needs require continuous monitoring.
7. The training officer of an agency is a professional with a responsibility to assist supervisors in solving training problems.
8. Many of the self-development steps important to the supervisor's own growth are equally important to the development of peers and subordinates. Knowledge of these is important when the supervisor consults with others on development and growth opportunities.

VII. HEALTH, SAFETY, AND ACCIDENT PREVENTION

1. Management-minded supervisors take appropriate measures to assist employees in maintaining health and in assuring safe practices in the work environment.
2. Effective safety training and practices help to avoid injury and accidents.
3. Safety should be a management goal. All infractions of safety which are observed should be corrected without exception.
4. Employees' safety attitude, training and instruction, provision of safe tools and equipment, supervision, and leadership are considered highly important factors which contribute to safety and which can be influenced directly by supervisors.
5. When accidents do occur they should be investigated promptly for very important reasons, including the fact that information which is gained can be used to prevent accidents in the future.

VIII. EQUAL EMPLOYMENT OPPORTUNITY

1. The supervisor should endeavor to treat all employees fairly, without regard to religion, race, sex, or national origin.
2. Groups tend to reflect the attitude of the leader. Prejudice can be detected even in very subtle form. Supervisors must strive to create a feeling of mutual respect and confidence in every employee.
3. Complete utilization of all human resources is a national goal. Equitable consideration should be accorded women in the work force, minority-group members, the physically and mentally handicapped, and the older employee. The important question is: "Who can do the job?"
4. Training opportunities, recognition for performance, overtime assignments, promotional opportunities, and all other personnel actions are to be handled on an equitable basis.

IX. IMPROVING COMMUNICATIONS

1. Communications is achieving understanding between the sender and the receiver of a message. It also means sharing information -- the creation of understanding.
2. Communication is basic to all human activity. Words are means of conveying meanings; however, real meanings are in people.
3. There are very practical differences in the effectiveness of one-way, impersonal, and two-way communications. Words spoken face-to-face are better understood. Telephone conversations are effective, but lack the rapport of person-to-person exchanges. The whole person communicates.
4. Cooperation and communication in an organization go hand-in-hand. When there is a mutual respect between people, spelling out rules and procedures for communicating is unnecessary.
5. There are several barriers to effective communications. These include failure to listen with respect and understanding, lack of skill in feedback, and misinterpreting the meanings of words used by the speaker. It is also common practice to listen to what we want to hear, and tune out things we do not want to hear.
6. Communication is management's chief problem. The supervisor should accept the challenge to communicate more effectively and to improve interagency and intra-agency communications.
7. The supervisor may often plan for and conduct meetings. The planning phase is critical and may determine the success or the failure of a meeting.
8. Speaking before groups usually requires extra effort. Stage fright may never disappear completely, but it can be controlled.

X. SELF-DEVELOPMENT

1. Every employee is responsible for his own self-development.
2. Toastmaster and toastmistress clubs offer opportunities to improve skills in oral communications.
3. Planning for one's own self-development is of vital importance. Supervisors know their own strengths and limitations better than anyone else.
4. Many opportunities are open to aid the supervisor in his developmental efforts, including job assignments; training opportunities, both governmental and non-governmental -- to include universities and professional conferences and seminars.
5. Programmed instruction offers a means of studying at one's own rate.
6. Where difficulties may arise from a supervisor's being away from his work for training, he may participate in televised home study or correspondence courses to meet his self-development needs.

XI. TEACHING AND TRAINING

A. The Teaching Process

Teaching is encouraging and guiding the learning activities of students toward established goals. In most cases this process consists in five steps: preparation, presentation, summarization, evaluation, and application.

1. Preparation

   Preparation is twofold in nature; that of the supervisor and the employee.

   Preparation by the supervisor is absolutely essential to success. He must know what, when, where, how, and whom he will teach. Some of the factors that should be considered are:

   (1) The objectives
   (2) The materials needed
   (3) The methods to be used
   (4) Employee participation
   (5) Employee interest
   (6) Training aids
   (7) Evaluation
   (8) Summarization

   Employee preparation consists in preparing the employee to receive the material. Probably the most important single factor in the preparation of the employee is arousing and maintaining his interest. He must know the objectives of the training, why he is there, how the material can be used, and its importance to him.

2. Presentation

   In presentation, have a carefully designed plan and follow it. The plan should be accurate and complete, yet flexible enough to meet situations as they arise. The method of presentation will be determined by the particular situation and objectives.

3. Summary

   A summary should be made at the end of every training unit and program. In addition, there may be internal summaries depending on the nature of the material being taught. The important thing is that the trainee must always be able to understand how each part of the new material relates to the whole.

4. Application

   The supervisor must arrange work so the employee will be given a chance to apply new knowledge or skills while the material is still clear in his mind and interest is high. The trainee does not really know whether he has learned the material until he has been given a chance to apply it. If the material is not applied, it loses most of its value.

5. Evaluation

   The purpose of all training is to promote learning. To determine whether the training has been a success or failure, the supervisor must evaluate this learning.

   In the broadest sense evaluation includes all the devices, methods, skills, and techniques used by the supervisor to keep himself and the employees informed as to their progress toward the objectives they are pursuing. The extent to which the employee has mastered the knowledge, skills, and abilities, or changed his attitudes, as determined by the program objectives, is the extent to which instruction has succeeded or failed.

   Evaluation should not be confined to the end of the lesson, day, or program but should be used continuously. We shall note later the way this relates to the rest of the teaching process.

B. Teaching Methods

   A teaching method is a pattern of identifiable student and instructor activity used in presenting training material.

   All supervisors are faced with the problem of deciding which method should be used at a given time.

1. Lecture

   The lecture is direct oral presentation of material by the supervisor. The present trend is to place less emphasis on the trainer's activity and more on that of the trainee.

2. Discussion

   Teaching by discussion or conference involves using questions and other techniques to arouse interest and focus attention upon certain areas, and by doing so creating a learning situation. This can be one of the most valuable methods because it gives the employees an opportunity to express their ideas and pool their knowledge.

3. Demonstration

   The demonstration is used to teach how something works or how to do something. It can be used to show a principle or what the results of a series of actions will be. A well-staged demonstration is particularly effective because it shows proper methods of performance in a realistic manner.

4. Performance

   Performance is one of the most fundamental of all learning techniques or teaching methods. The trainee may be able to tell how a specific operation should be performed but he cannot be sure he knows how to perform the operation until he has done so.

As with all methods, there are certain advantages and disadvantages to each method.

5. Which Method to Use

   Moreover, there are other methods and techniques of teaching. It is difficult to use any method without other methods entering into it. In any learning situation a combination of methods is usually more effective than any one method alone.

Finally, evaluation must be integrated into the other aspects of the teaching-learning process.

It must be used in the motivation of the trainees; it must be used to assist in developing understanding during the training; and it must be related to employee application of the results of training.

This is distinctly the role of the supervisor.

———

GLOSSARY OF TRAFFIC CONTROL TERMS

———

GLOSSARY OF TRAFFIC CONTROL TERMS

A

ACCESS ROAD - Public roads, existing or proposed, needed to provide essential access to military installation and facilities, or to industrial installations and facilities in the activities of which there is specific defense interest. Roads within the boundaries of military reservation are excluded from this definition unless such roads have been dedicated to public use and are not subject to closure.

ACCIDENT SPOT MAP - An area or installation map showing the location of vehicle accidents by means of symbols. Symbols may represent accidents classified as to daylight hours, night hours, injury or death.

ANGLE PARKING - Parking where the longitudinal axes of vehicles form an angle with the alignment of the roadway.

C

CENTER LINE - A line marking the center of a roadway between traffic moving in opposite direction.

COLLISION DIAGRAM - A plan of an intersection or section of roadway on which reported accidents are diagramed by means of arrows showing manner of collision.

COMBINED CONDITION AND COLLISION DIAGRAM - A condition diagram upon which the reported accidents are diagramed by means of arrows showing manner of collision.

CONDITION DIAGRAM - A plan of an intersection or section of roadway showing all objects and physical conditions having a bearing on traffic movement and safety at that location. Usually these are scaled drawings.

CORDON COUNTS - A count of all vehicles and persons entering and leaving a district (cordon area) during a designated period of time.

CORDON AREA - The district bounded by the cordon line and included in a cordon count.

CROSSWALK - Any portion of a roadway at an intersection or elsewhere distinctly indicated for pedestrian crossing by lines or other markings on the surface. Also, that part of a roadway at an intersection included within the connections of the lateral lines of the sidewalks on opposite sides of the trafficway measured from the curbs, or in the absence of curbs, from the edges of the traversable roadway.

D

DELAY - The time consumed while traffic or a specified component of traffic is impeded in its movement by some element over which it has no control usually expressed in seconds per vehicle.

DESIRE LINE - A straight line between the point of origin and point of destination of a trip without regard to routes of travel (used in connection with an origin-destination study).

DIVIDED STREET - A two-way road on which traffic in one direction of travel is separated from that in the opposite direction by a directional separator. Such a road has two or more roadways.

E

85 PERCENTILE SPEED - That speed below which 85 percent of the traffic units travel, and above which 15 percent travel.

F

FIXED-TIME CONTROLLER - An automatic controller for supervising the operation of traffic control signals in accordance with a predetermined fixed-time cycle and divisions thereof.

FIXED-TIME TRAFFIC SIGNAL - A traffic signal operated by a fixed-time controller.

FLASHING BEACON - A section of a standard traffic signal head, or a similar type device, having a yellow or red lens in each face, which is illuminated by rapid intermittent flashes.

FLASHING TRAFFIC SIGNAL - A traffic control signal used as a flashing beacon.

FLOATING CAR- An automobile driven in the traffic flow at the average speed of the surrounding vehicles.

FLOW DIAGRAM - The graphical representation of the traffic volumes on a road or street network or section thereof, showing by means of bands the relative volumes using each section of roadway during a given period of time, usually 1 hour.

H

HIGH FREQUENCY ACCIDENT LOCATION - A specific location where a large number of traffic accidents have occurred.

I

INTERSECTION APPROACH - That portion of an intersection leg which is used by traffic approaching the intersection.

L

LATERAL CLEARANCE - The distance between the edge of pavement and any lateral obstruction.

LATERAL OBSTRUCTION- Any fixed object located adjacent to the traveled way which reduces the transverse dimensions of the roadway.

LEFT TURN LANE - A lane within the normal surfaced width reserved for left turning vehicles.

M

MANUAL TRAFFIC CONTROL - The use of hand signals or manually operated devices by traffic control personnel to control traffic.

MANUAL COUNTER - A tallying device which is operated by hand.

MASS TRANSPORTATION - Movement of large groups of persons.

MULTIAXLE TRUCK - A truck which has more than two axles.

O

OCCUPANCY RATIO -The average number of occupants per vehicle (including the driver).

ODOMETER -A device on a vehicle for measuring the distance traveled, usually as a cumulative total, but sometimes also for individual trips, with an indicator on the instrument panel where it is usually combined with a speedometer indicator, or in the hub of a wheel in some trucks.

OFF-PEAK PERIOD - That portion of the day in which traffic volumes are relatively light.

OFFSET LANES - Additional lanes used for traffic which is heavier in one direction. Also known as unbalanced lanes.

OFF-STREET PARKING - Lots and garages intended for parking entirely off streets and alleys.

ON-STREET PARKING - The use of street and alleys (may be angle or parallel parking) for parking of vehicles.
ORIGIN DESTINATION STUDIES - A study of the origins and destinations of trips of vehicles and passengers. Usually included in the study are all trips within, or passing through, into or out of a selected area.
OVERALL SPEED - The total distance traversed divided by the travel time. Usually expressed in miles per hour and includes all delays.
OVERALL TIME - The time of travel, including stops and delays except those off the traveled way.

P

PARALLEL PARKING - Parking where the longitudinal axis of vehicles are parallel to alignment of the roadway so that the vehicles are facing in the same direction as the movement of adjacent vehicular traffic.
PARKING DURATION - Length of time a vehicle is parked.
PASSENGER VEHICLE - A free-wheeled, self-propelled vehicle designed for the transportation of persons but limited in seating capacity to not more than seven passengers, not including the driver. It includes taxicabs, limousines, and station wagons, but does not include motorcycles. (In capacity studies, also includes light reconnaissance vehicles, and pickup trucks.)
PASSENGER (TRANSIT) VOLUME - The total number of public transit occupants being transported in a period of time.
PEAK PERIOD - That portion of the day in which maximum traffic volumes are experienced.
PEDESTRIAN - Any person afoot. For purpose of accident classification, this will be interpreted to include any person riding in or upon a device moved or designed for movement by human power or the force of gravity, except bicycles, including stilts, skates, skis, sleds, toy wagons, and scooters.
PERCENT OF GRADE - The slope in the longitudinal direction of the pavement expressed in percent which is the number of units of change in elevation per 100 units of horizontal distance.
PERCENT OF GREEN TIME - The percentage of green time allotted to the direction of travel being studies.
PROPERTY DAMAGE - Damage to property as a result of a motor vehicle accident that may be a basis of a claim for compensation. Does not include compensation for loss of life or for personal injuries.
PUBLIC HIGHWAYS- The entire width between property lines, or boundary lines, of every way or place of which any part is open to use of the public for purposes of vehicular traffic as a matter of right or custom.
PUBLIC TRANSIT - The public passenger carrying service afforded by vehicles following regular routes and making specified stops.

R

REFLECTORIZE - The application of some material to traffic control devices or hazards which will return to the eyes of the road user some portion of the light from his vehicle headlights, thereby producing a brightness which attracts attention.
REGULATORY DEVICE - A device used to indicate the required method of traffic movement or use of the public trafficway.
REGULATORY SIGN - A sign used to indicate the required method of traffic movement or use of the traffic way.

3

RIGHT TURN LANE - A lane within the normal surfaced width reserved for right turning vehicles.

ROADWAY - That portion of a trafficway including shoulders, improved, designed, or ordinarily used for vehicle traffic.

S

SEPARATE TURNING LANE - Added traffic lane which is separated from the intersection area by an island or unpaved area. It may be wide enough for one- or two-lane operation.

SHOULDER - The portion of the roadway contiguous with the traveled way for accommodation of stopped vehicles, for emergency use, and for lateral support of base and surface courses.

SIGHT DISTANCES - The length of roadway visible to the driver of a passenger vehicle at any given point on the roadway when the view is unobstructed by traffic.

SIGNAL CYCLE - The total time required for one complete sequence of the intervals of a traffic signal.

SIGNAL CONTROLLER - A complete electrical mechanism for controlling the operation of traffic control signals, including the timer and all necessary auxiliary apparatus mounted in a cabinet.

SIGNAL FACE - That part of a signal head provided for controlling traffic from a single direction.

SIGNAL HEAD - An assembly containing one or more signal faces that may be designated accordingly as one-way, two-way, multi-way.

SIGNAL PHASE - A part of the total time cycle allocated to any traffic movements receiving the right-of-way or to any combination of traffic movements receiving the right-of-way simultaneously during one or more intervals.

SIMPLE INTERSECTION - An intersection of two traffic ways, with four legs or approaches.

SPEED - The rate of movement of a vehicle, generally expressed in miles per hour.

STOPPING SIGHT DISTANCE - The distance required by a driver of a vehicle, traveling at a given speed, to bring his vehicle to a stop after an object on the roadway becomes visible.

STREET WIDTH - The width of the paved or traveled portion of the roadway.

T

THROUGH MOVEMENT - (See THROUGH TRAFFIC)

THROUGH STREET - A street on which traffic is given the right-of-way so that vehicles entering or crossing the street must yield the right-of-way.

THROUGH TRAFFIC - Traffic proceeding through a military installation or portion not originating in or destined to that military installation or portion thereof.

TIME CYCLE - (See SIGNAL CYCLE)

TRAFFIC - Pedestrians, **ridden or he**rded animals, vehicles, street cars, and other conveyances, either singly or together, while using any street for purposes of travel.

TRAFFIC ACCIDENT - Any accident involving a motor vehicle in motion that results in death, injury, or property damage.

TRAFFIC ACTUATED CONTROLLER - An automatic controller for supervising the operation of traffic control signals in accordance with the immediate and varying demands of traffic as registered with the controller by means of detectors.

TRAFFIC CONTROL - All measures except those of a structural kind that serve to control and guide traffic and to promote road safety.

TRAFFIC CONTROL DEVICE - A Traffic control device is any sign, signal, marking, or device placed or erected for the purpose of regulating, warning, or guiding traffic.

TRAFFIC DEMAND - The volume of traffic desiring to use a particular route or facility.

TRAFFIC ENGINEERING - That phase of engineering that deals with the planning and geometric design of streets, highways, and abutting lands, and with traffic operations thereon, as their use is related to the safe, convenient, and economic transportation of persons and goods.

TRAFFIC FLOW - The movement of vehicles on a roadway.

TRAFFIC FLOW PATTERN - The distribution of traffic volumes on a street or highway network.

TRAFFIC GENERATOR - A traffic producing area such as a post exchange, parking lot, or administrative center.

TRAFFIC SIGNAL INTERVAL - Any one of the several divisions of the total time cycle during which signal indications do not change.

TRAFFICWAY - The entire width between property lines (or other boundary lines) of every way or place of which any part is open to use of public for purposes of vehicular traffic as a matter of right or custom. On military installation the word "public" refers to those persons having authorized access to, and use of, the common roadway facilities.

TRANSIT VEHICLE - A passenger carrying vehicle, such as a bus or street-car which follows regular routes and makes specific stops.

TRAVEL TIME- The total elapsed time from the origin to destination of a trip.

TURNING MOVEMENT - The traffic making a designated turn at an inter-section.

TWO-WAY STREETS - A street on which traffic may move in opposite directions simultaneously. It may be either divided or undivided.

TYPE OF ACCIDENT - The kind of motor vehicle accident, such as head-on, right-angle, etc.

TYPE OF SURFACE - The class of surface such as concrete, asphalt, gravel, etc.

U

UNINTERRRUPTED FLOW - The flow of vehicles under ideal conditions resulting in unrestricted movement.

V

VEHICLE - Every device in, upon, or by which any person or property is or may be transported or drawn upon a highway, except those devices moved by human power or used exclusively upon stationary rails or tracks.

VEHICULE OCCUPANCY - The average number of occupants per automobile, including the driver.

VOLUME - The number of vehicles passing a given point during a specified period of time.

W

WARNING SIGN - A sign used to indicate conditions that are actually or potentially hazardous to highway users.

WARRANT - Formally stated conditions that have been accepted as minimum requirements for justifying installation of a traffic control device or regulation.

ZONE (ORIGIN-DESTINATION STUDIES)$\underline{Z}$- A division of an area established for the purpose of analyzing origin-destination studies. It may be bounded by physical barriers such as rivers and highways, or may be the location of individual work organizations that have duty stations in relatively close proximity.

ANSWER SHEET

TEST NO. ____________ PART ______ TITLE OF POSITION ____________________________
(AS GIVEN IN EXAMINATION ANNOUNCEMENT - INCLUDE OPTION, IF ANY)

PLACE OF EXAMINATION ______________________________ DATE ____________
(CITY OR TOWN) (STATE)

RATING

USE THE SPECIAL PENCIL. MAKE GLOSSY BLACK MARKS.

1 A B C D E	26 A B C D E	51 A B C D E	76 A B C D E	101 A B C D E
2 A B C D E	27 A B C D E	52 A B C D E	77 A B C D E	102 A B C D E
3 A B C D E	28 A B C D E	53 A B C D E	78 A B C D E	103 A B C D E
4 A B C D E	29 A B C D E	54 A B C D E	79 A B C D E	104 A B C D E
5 A B C D E	30 A B C D E	55 A B C D E	80 A B C D E	105 A B C D E
6 A B C D E	31 A B C D E	56 A B C D E	81 A B C D E	106 A B C D E
7 A B C D E	32 A B C D E	57 A B C D E	82 A B C D E	107 A B C D E
8 A B C D E	33 A B C D E	58 A B C D E	83 A B C D E	108 A B C D E
9 A B C D E	34 A B C D E	59 A B C D E	84 A B C D E	109 A B C D E
10 A B C D E	35 A B C D E	60 A B C D E	85 A B C D E	110 A B C D E

Make only ONE mark for each answer. Additional and stray marks may be counted as mistakes. In making corrections, erase errors COMPLETELY.

11 A B C D E	36 A B C D E	61 A B C D E	86 A B C D E	111 A B C D E
12 A B C D E	37 A B C D E	62 A B C D E	87 A B C D E	112 A B C D E
13 A B C D E	38 A B C D E	63 A B C D E	88 A B C D E	113 A B C D E
14 A B C D E	39 A B C D E	64 A B C D E	89 A B C D E	114 A B C D E
15 A B C D E	40 A B C D E	65 A B C D E	90 A B C D E	115 A B C D E
16 A B C D E	41 A B C D E	66 A B C D E	91 A B C D E	116 A B C D E
17 A B C D E	42 A B C D E	67 A B C D E	92 A B C D E	117 A B C D E
18 A B C D E	43 A B C D E	68 A B C D E	93 A B C D E	118 A B C D E
19 A B C D E	44 A B C D E	69 A B C D E	94 A B C D E	119 A B C D E
20 A B C D E	45 A B C D E	70 A B C D E	95 A B C D E	120 A B C D E
21 A B C D E	46 A B C D E	71 A B C D E	96 A B C D E	121 A B C D E
22 A B C D E	47 A B C D E	72 A B C D E	97 A B C D E	122 A B C D E
23 A B C D E	48 A B C D E	73 A B C D E	98 A B C D E	123 A B C D E
24 A B C D E	49 A B C D E	74 A B C D E	99 A B C D E	124 A B C D E
25 A B C D E	50 A B C D E	75 A B C D E	100 A B C D E	125 A B C D E

ANSWER SHEET

TEST NO. _____ PART _____ TITLE OF POSITION _____

(AS GIVEN IN EXAMINATION ANNOUNCEMENT - INCLUDE OPTION, IF ANY)

PLACE OF EXAMINATION _____ DATE _____

(CITY OR TOWN)   (STATE)

RATING

USE THE SPECIAL PENCIL.   MAKE GLOSSY BLACK MARKS.

	A B C D E		A B C D E		A B C D E		A B C D E		A B C D E
1		26		51		76		101	
2		27		52		77		102	
3		28		53		78		103	
4		29		54		79		104	
5		30		55		80		105	
6		31		56		81		106	
7		32		57		82		107	
8		33		58		83		108	
9		34		59		84		109	
10		35		60		85		110	

Make only ONE mark for each answer.   Additional and stray marks may be
counted as mistakes.   In making corrections, erase errors COMPLETELY.

	A B C D E		A B C D E		A B C D E		A B C D E		A B C D E
11		36		61		86		111	
12		37		62		87		112	
13		38		63		88		113	
14		39		64		89		114	
15		40		65		90		115	
16		41		66		91		116	
17		42		67		92		117	
18		43		68		93		118	
19		44		69		94		119	
20		45		70		95		120	
21		46		71		96		121	
22		47		72		97		122	
23		48		73		98		123	
24		49		74		99		124	
25		50		75		100		125	